FASHION

INSIDE

OUT

DANIEL V'S GUIDE TO HOW STYLE HAPPENS FROM INSPIRATION TO RUNWAY & BEYOND

foreword by **Tim Gunn** photography by **Michael Turek**

WATSON-GUPTILL PUBLICATIONS/NEW YORK

Text copyright © 2008 by
DANIEL VOSOVIC

First published in 2008 by
WATSON-GUPTILL PUBLICATIONS,
an imprint of the Crown Publishing Group;
a division of Random House, Inc., New York.
www.watsonguptill.com
www.crownpublishing.com

Library of Congress Cataloging-in-Publication Data
Vosovic, Daniel.
  Fashion inside out : Daniel V's guide to how style happens from inspiration to runway and beyond / Daniel Vosovic ; photography by Michael Turek ; foreword by Tim Gunn.
  p. cm.
Includes index.
ISBN-13: 978-0-8230-3217-4 (paper over board : alk. paper)
ISBN-10: 0-8230-3217-5 (paper over board : alk. paper)
1. Fashion design—United States. 2. Clothing trade—United States. 3. Fashion designers—United States—Interviews. 4. Clothing workers—United States—Interviews. I. Title.
TT507.V68 2008   746.9'20973—dc22
2008016862
Printed in China
First printing, 2008
1 2 3 4 5 6 7 8 9 / 15 14 13 12 11 10 09 08 07

Photographs copyright © 2008 by
MICHAEL TUREK

Executive Editor: **JOY AQUILINO**
Development Editor: **AMY VINCHESI**
Art Direction & Design: **HSU + ASSOCIATES**
Designer: **MELISSA CHANG**
Production Director: **ALYN EVANS**

Watson-Guptill Publications books are available at special discounts when purchased in bulk for premiums and sales promotions, as well as for fund-raising or educational use. Special editions or book excerpts can be created to specification. For details, please contact the Special Sales Director at the address above.

Additional photograph credits: page 32: © 2008 by Diego Uchitel; page 65: © 2008 by Eric Ryan/Getty Images

To all those who aim to make this world a more beautiful place

Contents

Foreword

I FIRST MET DANIEL AT THE AUDITIONS FOR SEASON 2 OF *PROJECT RUNWAY*. HIS WAS A RARE EXPERIENCE: He had been before me and my

fellow three judges for about 30 seconds when we declared, "Congratulations! We're moving you forward to the next level." "Just like that?" Daniel responded. "No song and dance?" "You already did it!" I countered. And he had. His three garments were beautifully constructed and underscored the conceptual content of his portfolio: modern, sophisticated sportswear with just enough spirit of innovation to give them a fashion-forward thrust. As a mere enhancement of this first stage of the audition process, I suspected that the show's producers would consider Daniel to be adorable, and they did. Those qualities, combined with his sincere sweetness, ensured that he represented what we call "the complete package." So it was no surprise to me when he became one of our sixteen Season 2 designers. But it was indeed a surprise that he carried on to become one of the season's Final Three; that is, one of the three designers to show at New York Fashion Week and compete to be the winner. Why? Because of his youth and relative inexperience in the fashion industry.

At the time that we first met, Daniel was a few weeks shy of graduating from FIT. It's difficult and competitive enough to be selected as a semifinalist for *Project Runway,* but to be an about-to-be graduate of design school and be selected is almost impossible. I have the greatest respect for students and young designers. They are our future! But as is the case with all areas of art and design, maturity and coming into one's own takes time. I know from my experiences with my own students that the design, execution, and presentation of their senior year thesis collection represent a mere threshold, albeit a critical one, of work to come. Among my hundreds of students, I've only had a few whose design work at the time of graduation was beyond incubation:

the Proenza Schouler boys, the Vena Cava girls, and the Ohne Titel duo being some of them (and it's more than coincidental that they are collaborations). In his maturity of point of view and sophisticated spirit of innovation (trust me that "innovation" usually translates to clown clothes), Daniel personified that rarity.

Daniel didn't win *Project Runway.* Chloe Dao did. It was a tough competition among Daniel and Chloe and Santino Rice. Although they were impressed with Daniel's runway show at Bryant Park, the judges, especially Nina Garcia, cited Daniel's aforementioned relative youth and inexperience as being handicaps. They were concerned that these characteristics could potentially thwart his ability to meet the high level of expectation of the winner. I didn't disagree, but I felt horrible that issues beyond his control would bring him to a stalemate. Judge Michael Kors even offered Daniel a job: "Come work for me. Then, go out on your own." I was very moved by his generosity.

Owing to his success on *Project Runway* (he still holds the record for the designer who has won the most challenges) and the huge exposure offered by the show, Daniel was literally *thrust* into the professional fashion world and its related industries. Design school graduates take baby steps. Daniel was sprinting. His subsequent trajectory and corresponding success have exceeded expectations, and the pride felt by all of his colleagues and supporters is profound. He has more than matured into his own, as demonstrated by

the expansion and evolution of his design work and the scope and reach of his customer base. Furthermore, this book is a considerable milestone. I don't have the adequate words to express how thrilled I am that he chose to undertake this ambitious and formidable challenge. I'm especially pleased that this book is the work of a young designer in the American industry. Although this is a truly global industry, the American perspective is unique: We look at fashion through a lens of commerce. That's important, critically important in my view. Additionally, Daniel's relative youth serves him very well for this purpose. The fashion industry has undergone meteoric changes in the last decade, and Daniel is unencumbered by how the industry operated ten, twenty, or thirty years ago. If I had a dollar for every time I've heard an industry executive say, "We can't do *that*; we tried it twenty-five years ago and it didn't work," I could have retired by now. It's a new dawn and a new era, people!

Daniel devised *Fashion Inside Out* with thought and consideration for the industry needs of a new generation of future leaders. His perspective, investigation and research, and point of inquiry are exceptional and without peer. Using a broad base of experience and a wide spectrum of industry interviews, Daniel demystifies this complex and daunting world of fashion. I advise readers to brace themselves for an inspiring journey and a solid dose of education and insight. Enjoy!

Preface

FASHION DESIGN IS, AT ITS MOST BASIC, AN IDEA WRAPPED AROUND THE HUMAN BODY THAT CAN BE MANIPULATED INTO EVERY CONFIGURATION OF FABRIC, THREAD, AND EMBELLISHMENT IMAGINABLE. Fashion has become a massive global enterprise, a huge machine of commerce, celebrity, and trends that relatively few dominate but is undeniably shaped by countless individuals. It is one of the ways in which societies are remembered and recorded, and how historians consider how lives were lived. Our relationship to fashion is no different: the impact of our economic and environmental influences will someday be revealed by what we wear on our backs and hang in our closets. Fashion is then, now, and the future.

Fashion Inside Out presents the creative endeavor of fashion design from the designer's point of view. When I was first offered the opportunity to write a book about fashion, I was overwhelmed by the possibilities. I decided to focus on the design process because, regardless of a fashion designer's skill, taste level, or price point, inspiration must be gathered, ideas developed and refined, and garments created and presented—that much is certain for every designer. I begin the book with the crucial task of seeking inspiration, which in my view is just as significant to those who wear fashion as it is to those who create it: People don't necessarily need new clothes, but they do want to be inspired by them, as well as to wear them.

Much like fashion itself, this book is about style, method, and image, though it's also a great deal more. From drawing and draping to styling and selling, I take you through all the steps involved in creating fashion. I also share my own message and way of thinking as a designer with a collection I created just for the book. The line's sleek, modern styles come out of my original inspiration, allowing you to see an idea literally go from nothing to something—something I hope you find exciting.

Fashion Inside Out also explores how other creative people contribute to the process by taking their pieces of the puzzle and working them into the bigger picture the best way they know how. Throughout are interviews with some good fashion friends and colleagues who work in and around the industry—designers, editors, patternmakers, stylists, photographers, supermodels, and many other professionals—and who generously share their invaluable expertise and points of view.

Fashion design is obviously a very visual process, which is why I could think of no one better than photographer Michael Turek to document it. From cover to cover, this book features his absolutely stunning images, captured painstakingly over months of shadowing me in order to record my experiences creating the collection and my interactions with the experts.

To the uninitiated, fashion is mysterious (at best) and elitist (at worst). I hope that *Fashion Inside Out* sheds light on the exciting, demanding, and far-reaching process of getting next season's looks into your closet.

Daniel Vosovic

THE
INSPIRATION

WHERE FASHION BEGINS

FINDING INSPIRATION IS PERHAPS THE MOST CRUCIAL ASPECT OF THE FASHION DESIGN PROCESS. From the original spark, great ideas can ignite into grand visions, so that the designer's imagination intersects with the reality of fabric, shape, and fit and becomes something completely new and exciting. Designers seek inspiration from a variety of sources and then hone the ideas they unearth into garments or even entire collections. Simply flip through a fashion magazine or look at collections online to see the astounding diversity of inspiration from which designers draw their ideas.

URGENTLY SEEKING INSPIRATION

Many people ask me about inspiration: "Where do you find it?" "How do you transform inspiration into fashion?" "Are you ever afraid that you'll run out of things to say?" The most ridiculously random things have inspired me, from the sexually charged routine between legendary dancers Cyd Charisse and Gene Kelly in the 1952 film *Singing in the Rain* to Gwen Stefani in her "No Doubt" punk phase; from the sleek, clean lines of modern architecture to a single orchid arcing lazily on its stem. Inspiration can come from the most unexpected places, from immense to minute and everything in between; a very specific pattern on an old quilt or the vast richness of opulent eighteenth-century France can both be excellent places to start.

Having a place to sketch and mull over ideas is imperative for every designer, be it an office, coffee shop, or even at home. For me, this empty park, located in the Financial District, was the perfect place to flesh out the framework for my new collection, one that emphasized the fusion of technology and nature. Sitting encased in this pocket of green, with steel and glass towering overhead, was the ideal place to begin—everything started from here.

Inspiration doesn't need to be grand or glamorous; don't think that just because you don't live in a "fashion capital" you can't find inspiration in your own surroundings. Designers can be inspired by what's right in front of them: their daily routines, the tasks at hand, the people with whom they interact. When seeking inspiration, it's essential to persevere and push not only the level of design but also yourself and to persist in spite of distractions, inexperience, or a lackluster environment. It may at first be difficult to find things that are intriguing and stimulating in the day-to-day; a designer's eyes and mind may need to be trained to staying attuned—and open—to various stimuli. It's very easy to look at something and say, "I like it" or "I don't like it," but it's much more difficult to explain why. Getting out of one's comfort zone will hopefully provoke the mind to think outside the box and the eyes to see more than they would at first glance. Also, simply juxtaposing seemingly conflicting design elements may lead the design in a surprising and creative direction; soft and hard, rough and smooth, new and old, matte and shine—all of these are great design elements to consider when honing new ideas.

Finding inspiration should be a thoughtful process, a time for ideas to simmer and evolve. Unfortunately, during my time as a contestant on television's *Project Runway*, that wasn't really the case! The daunting words "thirty minutes to sketch" and "twenty minutes to shop" still ring in my brain. Day after day, week after week, my fellow designers and I were secluded from our usual daily life, forced to live without phones, television, radio, iPods, magazines, the Internet, or even the occasional walk in the park, and although this pressure cooker is great for TV, from a creative perspective, it can be counterproductive, to say the least. In fact, what viewers may or may not know is that most of the second season of *Project Runway* was taped in just twenty-nine days in back-to-back episodes. What was a week's time for viewers was in fact just a few hours to us, with no time to recoup after a fellow designer was "auf'ed"—just a wardrobe change, a quick meal, and back on the runway for the next challenge, given by the always effervescent Heidi Klum. When forced to scrape together idea after idea for each widely different challenge, without fresh inspiration or a release—especially in such a stressful situation—it became frustrating when we weren't able to fully flesh out the final designs shown on the runway because of lack of time. Nevertheless, it is a fantastic show, and simply watching someone sketch for two days certainly wouldn't be as entertaining, although it's important to be aware of the differences in how designers work in the real world.

Furthermore, at all design levels in the fashion industry, from JCPenney to Dior, designers must look for new inspiration for each new season; the difference is the extent to which they choose to use it. For example, say a high-end designer and a mass-market retailer were both influenced by similar trends and inspiration; the retailer would surely offer designs that are much more restrained and approachable, as they cater to the moderate-level shopper, possibly offering the new "color of the season" to an existing T-shirt collection or perhaps a bold print to one of their bestselling tops. The high-end designer, on the other hand, would most likely offer more saturated designs: embellishments, shoes, bags, and accessories—items where the original inspiration is more visible; two different customers moving at two different speeds.

The heart of the challenge in designing fashion is how to take that fleeting moment and channel it into a garment or collection.

Visual elements such as texture, light,

I was stunned by how the light played off the textures in this tunnel: combined with the graphic, horizontal lines, it created this beautiful, man-made sunburst effect. Having this "natural element" created out of sterile, cold cement further provoked my desire to combine unexpected fabrications and elements in my designs, hopefully with surprising results. Thankfully, Michael was able to capture the static energy of this passage that I was experiencing firsthand.

color, mood, shape, and movement are just a few of an original inspiration's characteristics that can be translated somewhat directly. For instance, the blending of colors on a flower's petals might develop beautifully into a floral print for spring dresses; the smoky, ashy hues from a chimney could be the beginning of a subdued color story; or the carefree ease of a dancer's performance could easily set the tone for an entire show, as when Alexander McQueen presented a collection on dancing models—spinning, twirling, and turning on a huge revolving dance floor in Paris—which heightened the mood of the clothing to the same carefree and fun feel as the environment in which they were shown. Or as when Michael Kors showed his dance-inspired collection on a traditional runway, complete with modernized iconic dancewear like wrap ballet sweaters, leggings, and tights.

The fashions and details of the past—usually identified by decade—have always been a jumping-off point for the new. Some of the biggest names in fashion have revisited the '20s, '40s, and '60s—virtually every decade of the twentieth century, as well as those from prior centuries. Drop-waist flapper-style dresses have come and gone more than once, and bell-bottoms have had more than their "fifteen minutes," but thank goodness we're over tight-rolled, acid-washed jeans and big hair—at least for now. There's a fine line between replicating something outright and using it as inspiration, but the past is there for designers to learn from and is one of the most important elements of their design education: knowing about what's come before and understanding why something emerged when it did and how those trends or details could work again in a new way.

A designer's education really never stops. Even after many years in the industry, fashion leaders will attest to still learning as they go, albeit a bit wiser than when they began, but still

learning. Whether designers obtain their education in a formal setting, such as a school course, through a hands-on apprenticeship or internship, or through self-taught lessons, it's imperative that they continually stay open to what's happening around them, throughout their careers, as inspiration can truly come from anywhere. Consider that while several designers may seek inspiration from the same source, the work of each one can evolve into something completely fresh and original through his or her own individual process, personal life experiences, and, of course, specific point of view.

For the collection featured in this book, I had two main sources of inspiration that I felt compelled to draw from: a fusion of technology and the eco-conscious movement that has been pushed to the forefront of today's society. I wanted to bring a softness to futurism—the clean lines, the harshness, the sterility—while giving eco-friendly fabrics and shapes a more modern, high-end feel. I'm a city boy through and through, and although I *love* the idea of mossy woodlands and towering redwoods, I often have to opt for Central Park and the occasional city park, inevitably surrounded by looming glass and steel. It got me thinking of how these two very different inspirations would work together, one clashing against the other to hopefully create something new and provocative.

As for whether I'll ever run out of things to say, I can answer that with a definitive "no!" I'll travel to the farthest reaches of the world to experience the most intense situations if I have to—*I'm never going to stop!* Well, at least I hope that's the case. For now I'll have to rely on what I have always relied on—my surroundings, my experiences, and my desire for thorough, in-depth research—and to be thoughtful and original about interpreting what I gather.

The internationally renowned artist Roxy Paine's installation "Conjoined" was a sublime source of inspiration for me. The idea of creating something organic and natural out of something inanimate and manufactured was not only interesting on its own, but setting it in the ever-evolving landscape of New York City made it even more so. "Enclosed nature" was a thread I wanted woven throughout my collection, the idea of a thing growing and expanding out of something that could no longer contain it. This piece was on display throughout the summer and fall of 2007 and has unfortunately already been taken down, which reinforces the importance of capturing inspiration in a moment . . . one never knows when it will come.

Before I leave my apartment, I always make sure I've packed my digital camera. Even if I'm not searching for a source of inspiration right then, the camera always comes in handy as a way to catalog images that have jumped out at me. It enables me to create an index of ideas to revisit and use if and when they're needed. If Roxy Paine's work hadn't spoken to me at this moment, I could always revisit it for another project or collection in the future.

TODD OLDHAM

TODD OLDHAM IS AN AMERICAN DESIGNER WITH A RICH, VARIED RÉSUMÉ. His creative genius has covered fashion, interior design, photography, stage and film wardrobes, a home and dorm room line for Target, and a home furnishings collection for La-Z-Boy. Todd was recently the host of Bravo TV's *Top Design* and is currently design creative director at Old Navy. Sitting down with Todd was a special treat for me, having been a fan of his work since the early '90s. With his vast design experience and technical know-how, Todd stressed to me the importance of inspiration and always looking forward.

DV: Fashion, interiors, furniture, books . . . is there anything you don't do?! Where does this desire come from—all of these ideas?

TO: Inspiration is clearly the most important spark of any effort, whether it's a business-minded effort or a creative effort, or how they merge together. So that has to be there, and the way one accepts inspiration is really about having a point of view. And if you have a very open mind and discerning taste, it's also really important to be a fan and to be able to see the beauty and the joy in lots of things, and then you're just constantly ripe and rich with inspiration. Whether you're seeing literal things that say, "God, that orange is magnificent and I love it and I want to do something with it," or you just recognize you're in proximity to passion. That is just as liberating.

DV: Have you always had that sense of awareness, or have you had to teach yourself to look, to train your eyes and your mind?

TO: I've always had it.

DV: Do you think everyone does?

TO: Yes, I do think everyone does have it. I don't think that you're trained to see it. It's these brackets that are slapped on by our methods, our parents, or whatever pipelines are influencers, and every little bracket you slap on yourself narrows your vision, and who wants narrow vision? A really open mind is the most essential tool.

DV: Where have you looked for inspiration?

TO: I'm a fan of all kinds of creativity, so since I'm really not much of a soothsayer I can't really see into the future all that well, so I admire what is done. I think you can be a fan and appreciate these things without being stuck in reproduction or retro-leaning ideas.

DV: Do you catalog your ideas, or do you literally just act on them right then and there?

TO: I act very quickly. I draw really fast. Everything's really fast and then I have to move to something else. I don't think I have A.D.D.; I don't have that affliction, but I do have the leaning.

DV: So you don't really go back and perfect?

TO: No, I don't go backwards at all. Even though I'm a fan of what's come before, I never look backwards.

DV: So say an idea hits you . . . orange. Orange is what you want to do. How do you go from color to something original? How do you translate an idea?

TO: Well, I keep saying, "be a fan." Be thirsty for the information because you can't make yourself interested in things. If you can somehow spark that passion where you have to know, it's like a crazy, joyous ride to be able to have a spark of an idea and watch it run through your head and turn into a million things. So once you get an idea, you learn how to bracket it, because you have to be really open-minded; things just can't float in the ether forever. It's just soup. So you have to kind of figure out ways to take chunks of it and put it together, but I think it just reveals itself. It's about not thinking. As soon as I start thinking, I screw stuff up.

DV: I often get inquiries from young designers asking where they should go to school, what classes to take, etc. In school you're taught the rules, guided by the norm, and then told to think outside the box. I was educated in a more regimented school setting, and I wonder what it would have been like if I had just figured things out on my own.

TO: That's why I'm not too keen on going back to fashion school. It's a huge blessing to get the knowledge of patternmaking and those kinds of things, and history will make you as rich as possible. I don't mean with money. It could make you rich in spirit, and that stuff is magnificent. But fashion is one of the fastest-changing machines, so if you're teaching anybody how to be a good designer, or a marketable designer, it's probably an old idea at that point. So just learn the technique and ignore the rest and get out.

DV: There are countless ways to become successful, and to find happiness in what you love. I wish I could impress more upon young designers that you don't need all of these "things" in order to be successful.

TO: Oh, absolutely. I never had any money or resources, and that never got in the way! I hear people say, "Oh, I need a backer." That's bullshit. The one thing you do not need is a backer. When I was starting I borrowed fifty bucks from my parents for fabric and I made something and I sewed it and I got five hundred dollars back, and I paid them back and then I was able to borrow a little more. It was just little incremental things that built up. I never had a backer, and it worked out really well. And I don't come from a rich family at all. It was all just common sense.

DV: Your mind and creativity over your wallet.

TO: Exactly. I mean, I sewed every piece of production for a couple years, my mom and I. You just do what you have to do.

DV: Absolutely. Regarding execution, can you discuss some different techniques in producing sportswear?

TO: Well, I'll tell you how I learned about it—from being pretty broke as a kid and shopping at Salvation Army. It worked out well with my budget, but I was *happy* to be there because to me it was like being in a couture salon. It was all one-offs, and they were incredible things. And they were made way better than anything I could afford. So I learned from buying their shirts, always too big, and taking one apart and putting it back together. To students I'd say, go buy an old, beat-up jacket from the forties and pull it apart, look at things that you've never seen before, look at why there are hidden stitches holding two pieces of interfacing together that you never see. That's the best way to learn all about sportswear. Cut it apart and then try to put it back together. Knitwear is great. Knitwear is one of the most fun things you can do, whether it's just chopping up knitted fabric because it's so forgiving, and it doesn't unravel. You don't have to hem it. It's one of the most wonderful ways to jump into design. And even if you're just cutting a plain T-shirt on the bias, just watch how it changes.

Also, if you can get hired into doing alterations somewhere for a few months, I seriously urge you to do it. I worked at Ralph Lauren in alterations for three months in Dallas, where I learned unbelievable amounts of stuff from sitting in the back with three big Southern ladies who would tear their wigs off because it got so hot.

DV: Ha ha! Moving on to eveningwear, I do like that the definition of eveningwear is changing. Yes, we still see mermaid gowns and sweetheart necklines, but I feel that the idea of dressing up is evolving, and more people are taking risks.

TO: Eveningwear for a designer I think is probably the most fun to do because you get to think in bigger expanses.

There's just a lot of freedom in it. It's really where you can cut loose as a designer and get away with more ridiculous ideas, less practical things, crazy prices, you know? It's a lot of fun in an endlessly diminishing market.

DV: Would it be an understatement for me to say that you have an appreciation for couture and handwork?

TO: Yeah, absolutely. I know all the rules and you can learn from them in an amazing way, but couture has moved into some other stratosphere of luxury—and I don't mean the price tags or the materials, but the idea that an artisan can express himself in such pure, extravagant ways and be appreciated. It's really a remarkable thing to see, especially when it's in the hands of people like John Galliano or Alexander McQueen; it's astonishing, old Saint Laurent stuff, you know? When it's in the right hands it's really something.

DV: I remember when I was at the Chanel studio in Paris; I don't speak any French, and I was in the sewing room working with seamstresses who were fifty-plus years old who had obviously been working there for years, and I was looking at this half-beaded tunic and really trying to understand how the heck this woman was doing it. She leans over, trying to show me how it works, and I think I got it. As I'm leaving I feel a little tug on my shirt; she's only up to my chest, and she just pours these beads into my hand and I started tearing up! I gave her this huge hug. It was absolutely beautiful.

TO: To be in the presence of those artisanal hands is really astonishing. It's a lost art. It's seriously diminishing. I mean, I don't know any young sewers that are going into it.

DV: And really understanding it.

TO: Yeah, it has to be in your DNA. It has to be passed down. It has to be the stuff that you grew up with.

DV: Are there any last things you'd like to mention or discuss? You obviously portray a positive message in all of your work, which I find quite infectious and admirable.

TO: It's just your attitude. You can get there by whatever path you choose. But the thing that's really important to tell everybody is this: Don't listen to anybody. Don't listen to me, don't listen to you; listen to yourself. Forge new pathways.

SKETCHING ESSENTIALS

Basic Sketching Tools

I carry a journal, a digital camera, at least one sketchpad, and an assortment of pens and pencils with me at all times. I can't stress enough how important it is to have tools at your fingertips so that you're able to record any loose thoughts or fleeting ideas at a moment's notice. I find that I'm rarely able to dictate where and how creativity will hit me, so it's best to be prepared.

I have quite a few journals, actually: One is a small (4 x 5 inches), unlined, lovely thing, handmade by my good friend Ethan (a fantastic photographer you'll meet on page 134). It's small enough to carry in my bag but large enough to allow me to make a decent-size sketch, tape in a fabric swatch or magazine tear sheet, or simply jot down my thoughts. It was just right for sketching a subtle sleeve detail I spotted while waiting in line at the post office or for writing down the address of a great new trim store a friend had stumbled upon; honestly, you just never know. I also have a larger sketchbook. A nice 11 x 14-inch size is usually large enough for detailed sketches and is still manageable for photocopying and passing around. I advise staying away from spiral-bound notebooks and hardcover journals, which are both difficult to hold and whose bindings make it difficult to write on both sides of a sheet of paper.

I also avoid super soft pencils or chalk, both of which smudge very easily. A sketching tool is obviously a personal choice, but I've come to the realization that when I use a soft lead (2B or softer) in a sketchbook that gets tossed around a lot, it makes it difficult to decipher details later. This can be a huge pain, as the whole point is to document ideas as they come so that you can access them whenever you need to—months or even years later.

Sketching Fashion

The basic proportion in fashion sketching is "nine heads," which refers to the height of the figure. Compare this to a realistic figure, which is traditionally seven heads tall. Drawing fashion figures taller, leaner, and more seductive in line lends an air of grace and sophistication to the figure, as well as to the clothing, as these are qualities envied by a majority of men and women. Another aspect to consider is the *balance line*, which indicates the figure's stance or movement, usually with weight more on one leg more than the other, walking, jumping, or dancing. The balance line extends straight down from the indent at the base of the neck to the floor. Even when drawing figures in a side pose or from the back, indicating a balance line will help keep them looking realistic and centered. Although all designers sketch differently, I find it easiest to start from the top and work my way down, making sure to use soft, swift strokes, keeping in mind that I will go back and define my lines later.

There are some excellent books that serve as in-depth guides to the specialized field of fashion sketching, but because you were nice enough to buy my book, I figured I'd include some basics to get you started. If this is your first time drawing fashion but you have some experience drawing still lifes or live models, it will seem odd at first that the figures are so elongated. If this is your first time drawing anything at all . . . well, my best advice is simply to just start. Don't be self-critical, and don't try to erase and start over—just let it flow. This is not about making perfect representational drawings; it's about getting comfortable with your pencil and translating your ideas to paper. So I suggest making yourself complete a certain number of sketches each time you pick up your pencil, and if you become frustrated and want to quit, at least push through the number you set for yourself (I think ten is a good place to start), as this will help you see the evolution of your skills each time you try.

This brings me to probably the *most* important rule of sketching (drum roll, please): *Never use an eraser.* Yup, that's it. One of the precious nuggets of gold that were handed down to me and now I'm passing on to you. This is especially important when starting out: It's essential that every designer learn from his or her mistakes, mistakes he or she won't be able to see if they were erased. Using tracing paper to sketch is also a great and much more cost-efficient way of sketching while perfecting your figures, as it allows you to trace over the parts that work and change those that don't. Yes, your figures may end up looking like deformed circus performers, steroid-ridden swimmers, or—worse yet—normal, proportionate human beings, but you must persevere! Overall, I find it most effective to sketch freehand on a single page, over and over and over again, taking one idea and allowing it to grow and develop into something slightly different, as each sketch becomes a variation of the previous one. Practice *does* make perfect. Luckily, family and friends simply love getting personalized sketches of stick figures as presents. Believe me, sketches have gotten me through more than a few holidays while I was on a budget.

The first step in understanding proportion when sketching fashion is the fashion *croquis.* A "croquis" literally means a quick sketch, or to "rough out." The overall proportion of a figure is the equivalent of nine heads stacked on top of each other, so the basic fashion croquis breaks down the body into heads. In general it's easier to think of the body as a collection of shapes—rectangles, trapezoids, ovals, and squares—and to then chip away the excess to show muscle and shape. When sketching, use a very light hand and short, fast strokes. Pay close attention to general

Basic Croquis

- **Start by drawing your balance line—a 90° angle down the center of the paper—and dividing it into nine equal segments. Then lightly pencil in the head and neck (1 ½ heads).**
- **Draw in the shoulder line. Create the bustline and torso (2 heads).**
- **Draw the waistline. Draw the hips and crotch (1 head).**
- **Draw the legs (4 ½ heads). Draw the feet (1 head in heels).**
- **Draw the arms and hands, keeping in mind that, generally, the elbow hits at the waistline and the wrist at the crotch.**
- **Place all appropriate style lines (princess seams, waistline, neck, etc.)**
- **Repeat these steps until the croquis is in proportion and looks balanced.**

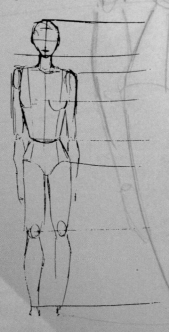

shapes and muscle features but also to the subtle details of form and pose, whether you're referencing pictures, magazines, or a live model.

Once you've become familiar with the basic fashion croquis and you have a feel for the body's general proportions, you can move on to the stylized fashion croquis, which is when you introduce poses and attitude to your sketches (I take you through a typical stylized croquis on pages 18–19). The *attitude* of the figure is very important. There is a slew of poses that are usually associated with certain categories of the fashion industry: the traditional hand on hip, a straightforward pose for sportswear; an über-chic and wispy posture for couture; an action shot for performance wear, etc. Although every designer has his or her own style of drawing, the most important thing to remember is that you're trying to convey a message, create excitement, and tell a story with your sketches. Is your clothing (and therefore your customer) whimsical and flirty? Haughty and sensual? Beautifully tousled? The poses, the style of the hair and accessories, and the color, format, and overall presentation of your figures should all reflect the message of the clothing and work cohesively to support your point of view. It's like wearing an evening gown with sneakers: Each element is ideal for its intended role, but together they don't convey a consistent message. When designers are working on their own, these rendered sketches provide a clear and consistent path to follow and reference while they work throughout the design process. At larger fashion houses, these sketches will be used for design development, constantly posted on design boards, discussed, removed, edited, and reposted for all those involved in designing to keep consistent with one another's ideas for color, texture, mood, and details of the collection.

Every designer should take a life drawing class. Although the proportions of a fashion figure are different, studying how the human body moves and poses will help you make a more realistic translation onto paper. It's so important to note the finer details, such as limb proportion, the inner skeletal and muscular system, and how the slightest shift in weight affects the rest of the body. Studying and rendering these practiced gesture drawings and subtle indicators of mood will unquestionably go a long way toward making your fashion figures more authentic. If classes aren't an option, set yourself up in front of a mirror or ask a friend to pose for you.

It's only because I love you and I know you would never use it against me that I've included one of my very first fashion sketches, completed within the first few weeks of fashion school. Man, I'd hate to meet her in a dark alley or—with those shoulders—in a lap pool!

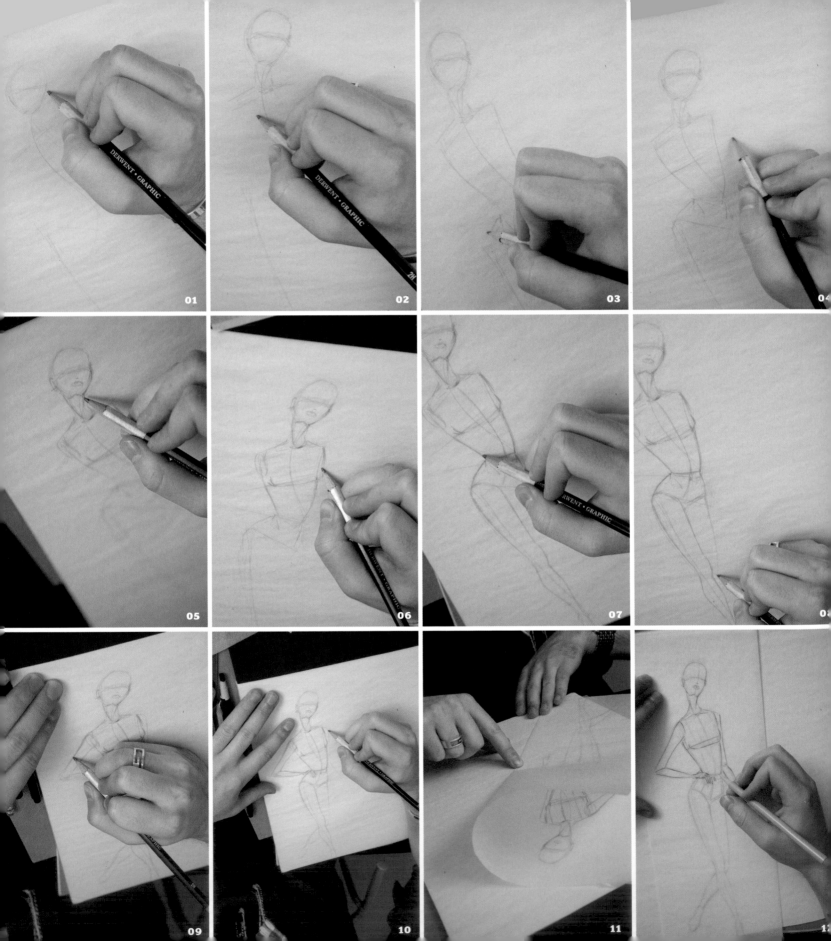

Stylized Fashion Croquis

When beginning the stylized croquis, I find it easiest to use a magazine tear sheet of a model in a tight outfit or a bathing suit to really study how the body moves. I would recommend using Gisele Bündchen's body from almost any photo shoot as a reference point; the sexy poses from a Victoria's Secret catalog are also a great reference in giving your figure some movement and life.

1. **Start by drawing your balance line: a 90° angle down the center of the paper.**
2. **Keeping the same proportion as the basic croquis drawn on page 17, lightly draw the head and neck** *(figs. 01-02).*
3. **Lightly pencil an action line—a guideline that shows which way your figure is moving, where her chest pushes in or out, and where her hips are going. A good rule is to create a shape that bends on one side and stretches on the other, like an S** *(fig. 03).*
4. **Draw the bustline, waistline, and crotch line as guidelines for how to shape your figure along the action line** *(fig. 04).*
5. **Draw the torso, waist, and hips** *(figs. 05-06).*
6. **Draw the legs in the position appropriate for your figure's pose, paying attention to the overall balance** *(figs. 07-08).*
7. **Draw the arms** *(fig. 09).*
8. **Place all appropriate style lines** *(fig. 10).*
9. **Take a piece of tracing paper and place it over your figure. Trace the parts of the croquis that work and redraw the sections that need revision. Do this as many times as necessary until you have a complete, clean template with no extra lines to assure that you are sketching on only the best croquis. You can then keep the unused sketches and begin to stockpile an archive for future use** *(figs. 11-12).*

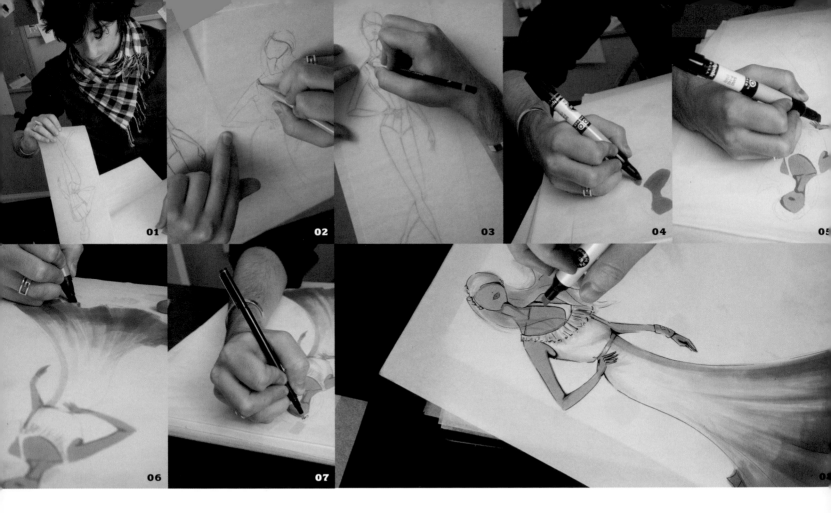

01 02 03 04 05
06 07 08

Fashion Sketch

Finalized fashion sketches can be completed with a range of tools, though I prefer to work with pencil and marker. Experiment with different techniques, as it can create some amazing effects: Rub a pencil over lace to add texture; use a white gel pen to create great highlights when rendering metallics or shine; or try layering various shading techniques to see which one gives the most depth.

1. **Place a piece of marker or tracing paper over your croquis** *(fig. 01)*.
2. **Take a hard lead pencil and very lightly trace over the croquis, keeping in mind the shape of your garment** *(fig. 02)*.
   (Tip: If you are having trouble seeing your croquis through the top sheet, a light box can be a helpful tool.)
3. **Lightly draw the outline of your garment and the hair, jewelry, and facial features of your figure** *(fig. 03)*.
4. **Take your fashion sketch and begin to add color, starting with skin tone first and then building up the color. When using markers, pull the color vertically in the direction of the garment, while paying attention to grain lines and movement of the garment** *(fig. 04)*.
5. **Add shading with pencil, a varying shade of marker, or by layering color** *(figs. 05-06)*.
6. **With ink or a darker pencil, go back and solidify anything that should be outlined** *(fig. 07)*.
7. **Add highlights with a white pencil or marker or gouache** *(fig. 08)*.

I try to work on an illustration as a whole, not focusing too strongly on one area at a time. Remembering to step back from my work to see it in its entirety helps to keep the figure balanced and proportionate.

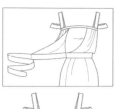

FLATS Although figures are an important part of fashion sketching, the clothing they don is even more so. Despite the undeniable beauty of a watercolor illustration of a woman riding a horse on a stormy beach, with the wind blowing her beaded evening dress, it fails to show how the dress is actually made.

Flats are exactly what they sound like: flattened sketches of a garment accompanied by all its specifics, including size, fabrication, and details such as trim and closures. They're a crucial part of the design process and an excellent way to sketch out a garment in a more controlled, thoughtful way.

So once there are some good ideas on paper, with the general ideas fleshed out on a fashion figure in a sketch, the next step is to translate them to more exact specifications—that is, onto a flat. A fashion figure is elongated and somewhat beyond average proportion, but a flats figure (when compared to a fashion figure) appears to be short and squat, almost as if a model was run over by a steamroller and flattened. It's important to remember that the garment being drawn is a mimicked version of what it would look like laid out flat on a tabletop, so the figure it's drawn on must also appear that way proportionately. It's not too difficult to translate the design from one to the other, but creating flats really means working the numbers: How wide is the lapel? Exactly how many buttons are on center-front? Precisely how long is the sleeve cuff? These questions and dozens more must be answered, and a flat must be precise because it will be sent to the manufacturer who will be producing the design, among other places. If so much as the smallest detail is left open to interpretation, it's the designer who will pay the price, not the manufacturer. If in that position, sometimes the manufacturer will do exactly what the designer would have asked for, but other times they will do the complete opposite. A sketch can give the general idea and feel of a garment, but a flat *must* be exact. The specifics can be a bit tedious, but once the general method is followed, the whole process becomes much easier to understand and work with.

Nowadays most flats are done digitally, with computer programs such as Adobe® Illustrator or InDesign that allow the user to create illustrations quickly and efficiently, whether it's a basic T-shirt or a tailored jacket with loads of detail. In fact, being a Technical Designer—someone who translates and executes the design sketches exclusively on a computer—is a great way to make money, be a part of the design process, and work in the fashion industry. Furthermore, good computer skills in general are highly valued in today's workplace, and the more knowledgeable and well-rounded a designer can be, the more his or her skills will be in demand.

But when designers are just starting out, or are working on their own, drawing flats by hand is a highly effective tool, as it forces them to think about all of the garment's details and requirements: How is it made? How does one get into it? What does it look like from the back? Believe me when I say that on more than one occasion, the question "So how do you get into it?"—whether asked of a student or a young professional, or even when casting for past seasons of *Project Runway*—has unfortunately been answered with an awkward silence.

Whether creating flats by hand or on a computer, if the design is symmetrical, remember that you only have to draw half of it and then mirror the image to make it complete. Adding the details comes next.

KARL ABERG

KARL ABERG IS A NATIVE OF SWEDEN who loves living and working in New York City. With a diverse background in the arts, Karl came to New York to attend Fashion Institute of Technology (FIT). He has worked as a designer within the American fashion industry for well over a decade, including stints for such brands as Polo jeans and John Varvatos. For the past six years Karl has been the men's design director at Marc Jacobs. Karl began sketching fashion figures and designing long before he was in a design room, but I admit it was comforting to hear that, before he landed at one of the most popular labels in the world, he hadn't always known what he wanted to do.

DV: What led you to where you are now?

KA: I always enjoyed drawing—that's how it started. I loved to draw when I was younger, and I would draw girls from magazines.

DV: So you were drawing fashion from the beginning?

KA: Yes, I didn't realize it was fashion drawing necessarily, or that it was design; I just enjoyed the drawing aspect. So after I finished high school in Sweden and went to an arts and crafts school for a year, I thought maybe I would like to be an artist or a painter. I had fabulous flashy friends at the time who were hairdressers and making money, so I thought that was the way for me. I became a hairdresser after that, and realized that maybe wasn't my calling because I still had that itch to do something, but I just didn't know how to do it in Sweden, how to become a designer. And that's why I think the idea of this book is really great.

DV: So how long did you do hair?

KA: Five or six years—three years of training and I worked for two. And then I heard about Central St. Martins [College of Art & Design] in London. I would have loved to go there because I love London so much, but I couldn't afford it. So a friend of mine told me about FIT, and in Sweden you can

get student loans for certain schools, and this was one of the schools that they had approved.

DV: Did you do the two-year program?

KA: Yes, and I thought it was both great and disappointing at the same time. It was not what I expected at all. It wasn't cool or fashiony, necessarily, and I didn't really realize that I had to learn to sew, which I wasn't very good at! That's not my strength, but it's great to learn it—I learned to use a seam ripper before a needle, because sewing goes fast! So when I graduated, I thought for sure I would work with women's wear because that's what I had studied. I was broke and kind of desperate to get a job, and then I got two offers: one was from DKNY to do women's bags, starting at the bottom. And the other was at Polo Jeans, doing menswear. I kind of switched back and forth between men's and women's a couple of times in the beginning of my career. For the last seven years I've been doing menswear. I'm happy that it turned out like that.

DV: What excites you now about designing menswear?

KA: I love that it's challenging to find something new in something that's already kind of there. You're not reinventing the wheel.

DV: Do you feel that there is less pressure?

KA: I feel like there's pressure in a way because there's a much narrower mark where you have to do something special, because guys aren't so open-minded as girls generally are. And that's very challenging in a way. I am also lucky where I am working now. I love it. I get to work on a product that I can relate to well.

DV: So after Polo you were led to Marc Jacobs?

KA: I had a few jobs in between. John Varvatos was just starting his line, and he was at Polo Jeans when I started. He was looking for somebody to help him out in the beginning, and then after three months I started working for him for two years.

DV: So there really is no right or wrong path—you saw opportunities as they came and didn't realize that you would end up where you are now. Did you just weigh the options as they came to you?

KA: Kind of. I knew I wanted to work for Marc even when I was living in Sweden. I was a hairdresser and he was always my top choice. So I think it helped me to have that as my dream. It does help to have a goal or an idea but to still be open to other things. It helps the more you know that you like a certain company or a certain type of product that you can zero in on it when you go to an interview; if you are interviewing at Polo your portfolio shouldn't look like Versace!

DV: Where do you look for inspiration and continue to pull ideas from?

KA: More than anything I just look at people on the street. There are so many cute people to watch—it's amazing! And I'm lucky that I do get to travel a bit because I see other cities too, other people. I'm in Florence a lot, and then we go to Paris and London. And then, for instance, in menswear there's a big movement that's been going on for a while with the '80s and '90s, the time when I was young; you just listen to that same kind of music and all these memories come back and that plays a big role in the inspiration, too. Sometimes you don't want to be too retro, but there's an element of that. Fabrics are really inspiring as well.

DV: Meaning you get inspired by fabrics and that dictates the design? Or vice versa? Or does it really just depend for every garment or collection?

KA: It really depends. Some just break through, like these cool, really lightweight nylons, and then it's limiting what you can do with them. At times you want to do something with volume or something really snug. In general I just try to think of a character for the season: "Who is that boy? Does he need a tweed suit or a flannel suit? Does he wear a sweatshirt, and is it bright or is it washed out?"

DV: Do you start asking those questions at the beginning of or throughout the design process?

KA: Throughout the whole thing. When I'm sketching I feel like I have a little relationship with that stick figure for five minutes.

DV: Yes. He talks to you, you talk to him!

KA: Yeah! It's fun.

DV: How does the design process work for you at Marc Jacobs? Are you given an exact inspiration or are you free to bring your own ideas to the table?

KA: I think it's unique in this company because it's pretty open. We have huge freedom, but sometimes it can backfire because you find out way too late that something wasn't popular! But I think in general they don't want to do anything that would put you in a corner—they always encourage. I am really lucky. We don't really work with merchandisers or sales until the last minute, which I think is quite uncommon. I'm trying to learn every season what did or didn't sell so that it can be a successful collection. I think we all tend to look at what has been done the season before and take inspiration from that and go forward.

DV: You design the Marc Jacobs' men's collections and Men's Marc by Marc Jacobs. How many are on your team?

KA: I have two people, one for each line. For Marc by Marc we have a technical support team, and the other collection is licensed by an Italian factory, so we work with their staff.

DV: What are your feelings about having so much freedom as a designer?

KA: It can be really intimidating in a way because with the freedom comes a lot of responsibility, and you want people to like what you do.

DV: How has your personal vision, your design philosophy, evolved working for a larger brand? Do you feel that you're in sync with what both they and you want?

KA: Yes, I do. I was going through my old portfolio and it was funny to see: A lot of it is still the same stuff that I would sketch now, but the attitude has changed a little bit. It's a little more focused but a bit more brave when it comes to pushing the details.

DV: Do you have any advice to give to young designers out there?

KA: I think it's important to focus on trying to do a really good job where you are . . . which goes for everybody. I'm definitely not encouraging people to swallow their egos, but I think you have to be realistic sometimes, and I feel like a lot of young designers, and some of my friends who were once young designers, would say, "I can't do that" or "I'm not working there!" I don't see that going so far. I think it's great that they are strong in their opinions, but I think you can try to open the doors a little bit more without losing your sense of self.

DV: Is there anything else you can tell us about the design process?

KA: We work with stylists, usually throughout the whole season. There's somebody there that you can kind of ball your ideas with. I'm really fortunate to work with really great people who help to bring out the best in me—they keep pushing me and kicking my ass!

DV: It's always helpful to have a second set of trained eyes to guide you. Are you afraid at times of showing and sharing your work?

KA: Yes, absolutely, because it can be brutal! But you just have to go for it. I think it's good that it's not somebody who's in the company all the time; I can be stuck on the product, too close, and it's great to have somebody who

can take a step out, come back in, and maybe they don't remember everything we talked about and something new will pop out.

Regarding my personal vision, it definitely helps working for a company like this because I feel like I'm constantly exposed to so many different things from the art world or the music scene. This kind of company attracts a lot of different kinds of people and they're all really cool. We love hearing what's going on in their heads. That's been a great influence.

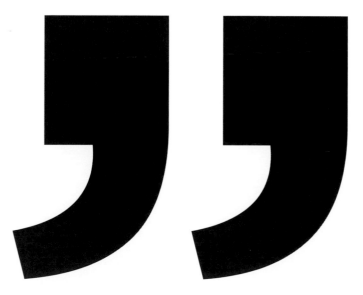

SWATCHING

You know the age-old question: Which came first, the chicken or the egg? **Well, the same question can be asked of fabric and its resulting garment. Fabric surely dictates a garment's design, shape, and fit, but if a designer is drawn to a particular silhouette or drape, it's likely that he or she will seek out the type of fabric that best supports it.**

For most designers, it's usually a combination of both fabric and silhouette that drives the selection process, with special attention paid to such variables as the upcoming season's trends, a customer's wants and needs, and, of course, the designer's vision. For instance, if you're aiming to achieve a sultry, vintage, boudoir-inspired collection, silk satin, antique lace, and silk chiffon come to mind, while heavy felted wool does not. The argument can be made that it's a clash of choices—the juxtaposition of the expected and the unexpected—that has created some of the most memorable and intriguing fashions. Regardless of which came first, fashion or fabric, it's vital that they work together seamlessly. (I know, I know . . . I'm a sucker for a good pun!)

When designers are looking to begin a new collection, they must first see what fabrics are available. If they are home-sewers and producing very small quantities and one-offs (one-of-a-kind pieces), it's fairly typical that they would be purchasing their fabric from a local retailer. The benefits of this option are the wide range of fabric options, face-to-face customer service, and essentially one-stop shopping. However, the lack of variety at some local fabric shops when searching for a specific fabric can become aggravating. Designers will be forced to pay retail prices since they aren't ordering directly from the supplier, which is the case when buying only a few yards at a time, unfortunately. On a larger scale, when design companies are looking to review fabrics, they will work directly with a fabric vendor, some of which represent up to six or seven different textile mills and who offer the latest and greatest fabrics being produced from all over the world. The designer can either go to the vendor's showroom, or a representative will bring "headers" to the designer's studio. Headers are large swatches of fabric (usually around 12 inches square) that show the pattern, fabric content, name of

As you can see, a good fabric store is literally filled top to bottom with options. I recommend making a few passes through before cutting any yardage, as you'll be able to see exactly what fabrics the store carries, and it may also turn up a fabric you didn't know existed!

the mill, weight, and all other pertinent information, as well as other available color combinations of the same fabric. It's a lengthy but necessary process, as considerations like delivery date and availability, cost, and appropriateness must be taken into account. Once these decisions are made, swatches and sample yardage are ordered, and then the editing process can begin. When you think of how many fabrics there are out there, and then add varying color combinations and pattern variations for each—wow, that's a lot of options! However, young designers don't have to worry about that massive editing process until they're working on collections with a wide range of designs and fabrications.

When shopping in fabric stores, it is possible to ask for a swatch of a specific fabric in order to take it around the store and easily compare it to similar fabrics or to take it home to think it over. More importantly, before a designer starts hacking away at a bolt of $80/yard fabric, he or she needs to be aware of the fabric store's swatching policies, which should be respected. If you're shopping for fabric, try to have at least a rough idea of what you're looking for, as walking into a room literally filled to the ceiling with options can be overwhelming. A notepad of observations made prior to a store visit can help keep you on track. When you've found what you're looking for, cut (or, if the store's rules dictate, ask someone to cut for you) a swatch that's large enough to show you the drape of the fabric and, if the fabric is printed, a full *repeat* (the entire pattern), but not so large that you're heading into actual yardage. Be sure to record the price per yard, the fabric content, the available yardage (especially if there isn't much on the bolt), and what store you saw it in. Taking the time to gather this information will allow you to compare your initial choices with those you may get from other stores. Buying fabric online is also a possibility, though not something I've ever done, or really heard of any designer doing. Seeing a fabric's true colors, feeling its texture, and noting its drape are things you can really only do successfully in person, although if an online store is able to provide a swatch book or sample yardage, that may be an alternative if there are no good stores in your area.

So, before you buy anything, here comes Golden Nugget of Knowledge/Fabulous Tip from Daniel #2: Take the fabric to the window . . . genius, I know. It's likely that the fabric store has horrible, nauseating florescent lighting, similar to that found in dodgy hotel bathrooms and sterile hospital hallways, which means it's probably affecting the true color of the fabric. Don't be shy about taking the bolt of fabric to the window or, after taking a swatch, going outside to look at it in the proper daylight. This is the only way you'll know how it will look in an everyday setting.

Also, if you're searching for fabrics for more than one design—say, for a wedding party—bring along copies of your sketches so you can "style" the looks as you search. This will allow you to compare all of the fabric possibilities for not just one design but for all of the looks, ensuring cohesion among the group. If I've designed a collection of dresses, for example, I sometimes copy and reduce the sketches of each dress in order to fit them all on a few more manageable pages and then record my initial thoughts on fabrics right next to them. This helps me stay on track and avoid becoming overwhelmed as I search through hundreds of options. **DV**

During *Project Runway*, time was of the essence during our trips to the fabric store: Sometimes we had as little as 15 minutes to shop. Here I'm reviewing fabrics with the incomparable Shahla and Raul at Mood Fabrics, two employees who quickly became friends and who were always willing to offer assistance or suggestions for alternative fabrics. A good store should have employees who are knowledgeable about their products: availability, location, content, and cost. They may also offer connections to people or services that a designer may be in need of.

‘

DIANE VON FURSTENBERG FIRST ARRIVED ON THE FASHION SCENE IN 1972, AND BY 1976 SHE HAD SOLD MILLIONS OF HER SIGNATURE WRAP DRESS. She came to symbolize female power and freedom to an entire generation by encouraging women to "feel like a woman, wear a dress." In 1997, Diane reemerged on the fashion scene with the re-launch of the Wrap dress. Today, DVF has expanded to a comprehensive line of sportswear, dresses, swimwear, accessories, cosmetics, Diane von Furstenberg by H. Stern fine jewelry, luggage, and a partnership with the Rug Company. In addition to her role as designer, Diane is the president of the Council of Fashion Designers of America (CFDA). Diane has always practiced what she preaches in her life and in her design philosophy. Despite her hectic schedule, she took a few minutes to illuminate the steps that have lead her to great success and to becoming the woman she knew she always wanted to be.

DIANE VON
FURSTENBERG

DV: Who or what inspires you in your work and in your life?

DVF: Women have always inspired me and I design to inspire them. I did not know at first I wanted to be a designer, but I knew the woman that I wanted to be. I became that woman while designing and giving women clothes that would give them the confidence I was looking for. From the beginning, I had this amazing dialogue with women. I was learning from them and sharing what I was learning.

DV: Which has been one of your most memorable collections and why?

DVF: My most memorable collection was the first one. I did not know what I was doing. I threw myself into the water, and showing a collection always feels like throwing yourself into the water!

DV: For young designers starting out, do you have any comments or advice on either major pitfalls to avoid or particular things to stay focused on?

DVF: My advice to young designers is to have a big dream, but take little steps. . . . Make sure you are true to yourself and go for it!

DV: Being named president of the CFDA was a huge accomplishment. What plans do you see implementing during your time in that role?

DVF: At this point in my life and career, it is about giving back and sharing my knowledge, my connections, and that is why I love my role as the president of the CFDA. I want to help others, create a strong network of designers and new talent, and make the members proud to be members.

THE
POINT OF VIEW

CREATIVITY MEETS CLIENT

KNOWING WHO YOU ARE AS A DESIGNER IS ESSENTIAL . . . and having everyone else know who you are as a designer is invaluable. There's no better way for a designer to make a definitive statement and a lasting impression on people than by ingraining who they are in every collection they design. A point of view is equivalent to asking, "What is your message?" "What is your aesthetic?" and "Whom do you design for?" A good designer can answer all of these questions and—more significantly—can show the answers in every garment that he or she designs. You may recall that throughout *Project Runway*, the astute Nina Garcia, former fashion director of *ELLE* magazine, asked the probing question "What is your point of view?" to almost every designer at one point or another. It's not the worst thing to be asked, but it does mean that the clothes don't speak for themselves, and in fashion, that is the ultimate goal. In most real-life settings, a designer cannot be on hand to explain his or her designs, so they need to stand on their own without explanation. Honestly, I have discovered that this is something designers either have ingrained in them naturally (for the most part) or have trained themselves to understand. At its most fundamental, a point of view breaks down to what a designer likes and dislikes, and every other style and design choice gets made from there

AN ESSENTIAL RELATIONSHIP

The relationship between a fashion designer and his or her client is a special one that can strengthen and define the image and message of both. Designers can look to their clients for inspiration, enthusiasm, and direction, while clients look to designers for those same things. It's extremely important for a designer to know and understand who his or her customer is, because an awareness of the customer's needs, expectations, and desires will lead to designs that are not just visually stunning but valued and useful.

Ever since she was a leggy young ballerina and I an aspiring designer, the lovely Anna Scott has been a constant source of inspiration and creativity to me—my first muse, if you will. She's an angelic beauty, a fiercely talented young woman, and one of my best friends, someone whom you'll be seeing quite a lot of in this book. I'm thrilled that I have her in my daily life here in New York City as a constant trigger for my imagination, but I'm exponentially even more thrilled that I get to introduce her to you.

There are countless examples of how a strong point of view and thorough knowledge and understanding of the customer have created lasting benefits for both. In some cases it's virtually impossible to differentiate a designer's drive to satisfy his or her own vision from the client's desire for something fresh and exciting. Every commercially successful fashion designer works with their particular "ideal" woman in mind: Ralph Lauren's is all-American and country chic; Miuccia Prada's is cerebral, progressive, and quirky; Donna Karan's is independent, bold, and urban. That said, there seems to be a cross-pollination of style with today's women, as it's increasingly rare for a woman to wear just one designer head to toe anymore.

Of course you don't always get to work with your ideal client. Some of the hardest *Project Runway* challenges involve designing for "real" women you've only just met and with whom you get to spend maybe thirty minutes exchanging ideas and information for a garment that best suits her. The most difficult part is that there is no "shopping" involved—no time to try different things and decide "that's not right for me"; it's very personal for both the designer and the woman, and you don't have the luxury of deciding whether it's the right fit for either of you. In a normal setting, a woman who likes Prada would be shopping at the Prada store, while the woman in the jeans and T-shirt and biker boots would be shopping at Levi's and her favorite leather shop. Neither would mistake the other's fashion comfort zone for her own, and there wouldn't be much overlap. Unfortunately, on *Project Runway*, "jeans and T-shirt" designers are forced to design for Prada-loving

...lients and vice-versa. Sometimes as a designer you are forced to deal with a customer who doesn't want your aesthetic, and you don't want theirs, either. On a reality television show, you do the best you can to find some common ground and make it work because you want to win the challenge! In the real world, the stronger your point of view, the more likely it is you will attract like-minded customers.

Without definition and a strong point of view, a designer's message gets lost, and the simple question "Who is your customer?" can be difficult to answer. I've always been drawn to bold, creative women as sources of inspiration (as well as aspiration): actors like Cate Blanchett and Jennifer Connelly, singers like Shirley Manson and Charlotte Gainsbourg, and the innovative editor of French *Vogue*, Carine Roitfeld (one of my all-time favorite style icons). Although they may not represent a single type of beauty, sexuality, attitude, or personal style, these women are all fashion-forward thinkers whose style isn't overwrought with rules and guidelines; for them, fashion is meant to be fun, uninhibited, and provocative. This is the type of woman to whom I aspire in my own designs. I've often said that perfection is overrated—it's okay to have a little dirt under your nails (metaphorically, that is). Women who are confident in how they dress and fearless when trying something new and possibly unconventional, regardless of whether or not others love it, rank higher for me than those who always play by the fashion rules.

One such woman, whom I've known since we were just teenagers growing up together in the suburbs of west Michigan, is my best friend, Anna Scott, whom

continually inspires me in new and unexpected ways. she served as both the muse to my collection and as my client for one very special garment. In exchange for contributing her thoughts, explaining her needs and desires, and for letting us photograph her in a leotard (!), I promised to design a party dress for her upcoming birthday soirée, a task that I couldn't take lightly, as it's always a fabulous party!

Whether a designer lives in rural Missouri or in midtown Manhattan, he or she should be aware of the style and fashion there and how that specific market translates into needs of the clients. Floor-length hand-beaded gowns may be a sure fit on Barney's 4th floor but would probably be superfluous at a small local boutique; on the other hand, a uniquely designed screen-printed hoodie could be well received in a smaller suburb but may be lost in a larger, heavily saturated market. Whether you're selling sweatshirts or cocktail dresses, finding the perfect balance between being acknowledged by the right client at the right time and being accessible to them is key regardless of the particulars of location and/or the product being offered.

If you're seeking to become a fashion designer, you should keep in mind that your point of view not only signifies who you are to your clients but it ultimately sets you apart from everyone else. Quite honestly, the world doesn't really *need* another fashion designer; there's surely enough clothing in the world to cover us all for years to come. But it isn't solely out of necessity that designers do their work—it's out of desire. People look to designers to help them play a role, evoke or heighten an emotion, and to help them communicate

TIM GUNN

TIM GUNN IS CHIEF CREATIVE OFFICER AT LIZ CLAIBORNE, INC. AS CCO, Gunn leads an ongoing campaign to restore a culture that welcomes the creative process and helps to shape a more competitive, consistent, and compelling product. Formerly, Gunn served as chair of the Department of Fashion Design at Parsons The New School for Design and was a vital part of the Parsons community for more than twenty-three years. Gunn has garnered critical acclaim and is a fan favorite in his role on the Emmy-nominated *Project Runway*, where he acts as mentor and sounding board to the budding designers. Tim shares his guidance and wisdom with all manner of eager audiences through many outlets. There is much more to the self-described "mentor and truth-teller" of the fashion industry, however, and having the chance to delve a bit deeper with him one-on-one was a delightful treat.

DV: To begin, what is your role at Liz Claiborne and what does that consist of?

TG: I'm chief creative officer, so I work with all the brands extensively. I'm a mentor for the designers. I'm a truth-teller. I'm a sounding board. I'm a therapist. I'm a spokesperson for Liz Claiborne when necessary, and I'm an advocate for design at the executive level. And the CEO, Bill McComb, who's an incredibly dynamic visionary, he's been here almost a year. I was his first hire, which I'm proud to say! He's built a whole new team, and it's all around what really is at the core of the whole company, which is irresistible product. And Bill says if we don't have irresistible product, we may as well not exist. So we're unshackling the designers—we are just saying, "Give us your all; don't feel held back."

DV: And do you work with any of the designers regularly? Is there any one-on-one interaction, à la *Project Runway*?

TG: I work more with the executive VPs over the brands, because the difficulty that I have, since the designers don't report to me, is I don't want to undermine anybody. I don't want to undermine the head designer. I don't want to undermine the creative director. So if I'm a partner with the big boss, then we do these things together for the most part. I'm also doing talent recruitment.

DV: What elements do you think distinguish fashion from clothing?

TG: Well, I say it all the time: We *need* clothes; we do not *need* fashion. We want fashion, we desire fashion, but we don't have to have it. We could navigate the world in really basic items of apparel, things that are just a front and a back. Fashion for me is born out of a context, and it's one that's societal, cultural, and historic, certainly, and it's economic and political—and because it's born out of a context, it's constantly changing by definition. Clothes don't need to change—they can just be the same season after season after season—but fashion will change by definition. And there are people who are very good clothing designers, but they aren't fashion designers. Then there are people who really understand the pulse of fashion, and they're able to gauge it.

DV: You studied sculpture in college, correct?

TG: I studied a lot of things. That was the thing that compelled me toward design . . . and I studied architecture briefly.

DV: So throughout your studies, your work, and from what you've been exposed to—whether that's on the outer fringe or being directly involved—what designers or collections or pieces have spoken to you?

TG: Architects were the first designers who really had an impact upon me. The early classicist Palladio to Frank Lloyd Wright—at least when I was younger.

DV: This whole book is about the process. We know Tim Gunn as chief creative officer and as adviser on *Project Runway*, but I want to know how you got here.

TG: Well, I was a Lego fiend. As a kid I couldn't get enough of it. I spent all my allowance money on Lego, and it was in the days before it was a prescription. I mean, today you buy it and there's a picture of something [on the box].

DV: And you can create only that.

TG: Yeah. And in my day, you would buy a box of white bricks, you'd buy a box of red bricks, you'd buy a box of roof tiles, you'd buy a box of windows, and as far as I was concerned, I just couldn't get enough of it. And then I'd take the whole thing apart—I mean, I actually would live with it for a couple of days and then take it apart and rebuild. I simply loved it. And it caused me to do a lot of research into different architectural styles and it also got me very interested in interiors because that was the next step—what goes in this structure? And I would do things like make curtains and make furniture and then I started making my own things, my own collection.

And then my grandmother gave me a calendar from France—it was twelve months basically of a different chateau, and it was elevations that you would cut out and put together assembled—you had a three-dimensional model of the chateau. It was really beautiful. Then I became obsessed with paper models and started haunting hobby shops and trying to find these things, and they could be very, very elaborate. So it just started this trajectory of making things.

DV: So from a French calendar and Legos, life took off?

TG: And I will also add, because it would be an omission if I didn't, I was enraptured with my sister's Barbies and their clothes. And when she would shop for Barbie's clothes, I always wanted to go with her. So I was an advisor . . .

DV: . . . even at that age. Helping and guiding, so to speak. So what are some of your favorite pieces of art? After years traveling the world quite extensively, what speaks to you now in art and in fashion? What still excites you?

TG: Oh, things excite me all the time. In art, it's really interesting, the work that used to put me to sleep when I was taking art history now I find exhilarating. And it's all the Renaissance painting. And I think it's the narrative storytelling element of it and the iconography—the symbols, I find fascinating. And in many cases I also find the scale *fascinating*: A lot of it's small and it's done in egg tempera, and I haunt those galleries at the Metropolitan Museum.

DV: Jumping to fashion, is there someone who really speaks to you that you can see every season?

TG: Well, there's historic and there's contemporary, and in terms of contemporary, I make a point of seeing what everybody who's showing is doing, and I do most of that online. I have developed a decided disinterest in things that aren't happening in this country.

DV: Really? Why is that?

TG: I don't disrespect it. I'm not particularly interested in it. I'm more interested in how American designers address fashion. And that's largely because of the additional dimension of problem solving that American designers engage in, which is that they look at fashion through a lens of commerce, and I have the greatest respect for that. I've had a lot of European people be critical of that statement and say that American design isn't creative, because of that. Well, if you think that American design in general isn't creative that's one matter, but if it's not creative, it's not because it looks at it through a lens of commerce—that's a limitation of the designer, or it's your point of view that you bring upon it. But to say that European design is unencumbered by commerce, perhaps that may be the case at its inception, but if the work doesn't sell, who cares?

DV: Absolutely.

TG: And for me the term "wearable art" is an oxymoron, so it doesn't interest me. But historically, I look at the twentieth century as really the beginning of fashion. For me the first truly seminal moment for fashion in the twentieth century, the launch of everything, was Coco Chanel. She realigned lifestyle when it was acceptable in the Western world. When you think about it, before Chanel, you couldn't let an ankle show. Suddenly women's calves are showing—I mean, talk about scandalous. Costume jewelry? What was that, other than stuff you'd play with? Suddenly it's all the rage. That was a hugely seminal moment. And I say this to my students— the world wasn't waiting for Chanel; it's just that Chanel woke up the world. It was a moment. And then we have World War II to thank for the rise of American fashion because all those couture houses closed in Europe. Suddenly we have Norman Norell and Claire McCardell and hugely important figures for American fashion for different reasons, and history, I keep saying for the Western world, was never the same. And it's very interesting when you look at fashion history—why is it so Western biased? It's very simple: Because in the Western world it changed constantly. In the East it remained the same for millennia. I mean the Korean hanbok, the Japanese kimono, the Indian sari, the Chinese cheongsam . . .

DV: That's an interesting perspective.

TG: So I do look at fashion through that contextual lens, and there are tons of people who excite me today. I love Fashion Week. From the incredible Diane von Furstenberg to the Proenza Schouler boys, Yeohlee Teng. I think one of the most underrated American designers is Charles Nolan. I think he's phenomenal.

TG: The game is completely different. In fact, I cite around 1987 to 1988 as really being a turning point for American fashion. Prior to that time, American fashion could be so clearly and narrowly defined, and at that moment it was Donna Karan, Calvin Klein, and Ralph Lauren—that was it. Everybody else was just like them. And then fashion went into this tailspin, and it didn't know what it was or what it was doing, and there was a crisis in retail, there was a crisis in design, and when it finally begins to come together again by the mid-'90s, it's a totally different fashion arena. Totally different and incredibly diverse, and it's become more and more diverse as we move forward.

DV: Which is thrilling.

TG: It's tremendously exciting. Now I don't think it will ever change, and people challenge me on that, and I say, "But wait a minute. The reason why I don't think it'll ever change is because the customer's not going to want to go back to a narrow swath. The customer loves the diversity."

DV: Fashion is much more accessible now, and whether that comes in from technology or other media, I completely agree that I don't think the customer will ever want to go back. What about young designers who chase trends?

TG: Well, I'll say that you need to have your radar up about it, meaning there are different ways of operating for a designer. There are people—and I'll cite Michael Kors in the most respectful way—who are really very trend aware . . . I wouldn't say that their work is trendy, but it's trend conscious. Then you have people like Anna Sui, who—

DV: I feel that now is a great time for design. I feel that people are so supportive of young designers, especially in New York, and that people are anxious, people want it.

TG: What concerns me is that as eager and as fervent a time as this is for young entrepreneurial designers, as much as this industry wants to prop them up and initially support them—it's just as eager later to topple them over. I mean people who won CFDA awards . . . it's like, where are they now? And that's the really scary thing, because it's one thing to *start* a career; it's another thing to sustain it. It's really a scary prospect, and one has got to be thinking long term and the long haul. You can't just be, "Oh, this season or next season." I'm not saying that they have to have anything designed, but just in terms of their business thinking and their projected planning, it's got

DV: Does her own thing.

TG: Right. And some seasons she's in and some seasons she's not. And right now she's in, and I have respect for both ways of operating. It's just a matter of what's right for you. But through thick and thin, I bring this up with my students all the time, with seniors especially, and the dialogue goes something like "What's the matter? Why are you drifting? What's going on?" "Well, I'm confused, I'm conflicted, I'm not certain what direction to go in with this collection." And my way of grounding them and getting them to focus is to ask one very simple question: "Who's the customer?" And invariably with someone who's struggling, they don't know. It's like, "Well, you need to know who the customer is. Who is going to wear these clothes?" Once you know that, it will help guide you and direct you. I'm not challenging you in asking that question by saying, "I don't believe you have a customer." Of course you do!

DV: You and I have sat through many hours of *Project Runway* auditions where people have a very difficult time answering that.

TG: Yes, that's very revealing. It can't be the first thing that's resolved, because I don't want it to encumber the creative process, but once the work's out there, then what?

DV: You want it on bodies, not just hung in a closet.

TG: Right!

DV: Do you have any thoughts on how people can get air in into this industry? Possibly to those young designers not living in New York, who don't have a support system of fashion-related people around them?

TG: The first thing is, you need to make something. You can't just sit around thinking about it. You have to actually experience the making process. I really believe people need to study fashion. I don't believe they can just be a home sewer and do this in a vacuum, because you know what's missing—the fashion . . . their clothes. Part of the studying is being in the community, where you have similarly impassioned people for whom this should be, "If I can't do this, I'm going to die," and to really engage in a dialogue about design. It's just critically important; otherwise, you just resign yourself to doing a bunch of granny circles. And if that's what they want to do—that's the difference between clothing and craft and fashion. I don't disrespect the other two, but they are in a different category; it's not fashion. So I would just say wherever you are, study it. There are fashion programs all over the country.

DV: And to me, that's not only in a more traditional setting. I know Todd Oldham spent three months in a Ralph Lauren alterations backroom studying how garments are made, taking them apart, etc.

TG: You need to know that.

DV: So when you say "study it, experience it," it's not solely in a structured environment like school?

TG: Oh, yes. If you're working in a tailor shop and that's your real experience, then you know how to make clothes. Then I would say to everybody, take a fashion history course, take an art history course, take a design history course. Wherever you study, you get out of it what you invest into it.

DV: It's absolutely what you make of it.

TG: A designer needs to bring more to this experience than I do, and want it, be hungry, research . . .

DV: I think having a great product and the knowledge is necessary, but it really is only part of the package.

TG: You have to make the product known. It's not going to attract an audience unto itself.

DV: There's no right or wrong way to do things. I think that's the broad point. Just have a hunger for it and go after it.

TG: And be tenacious, and be undaunted by all the difficulties and the rejections. If you have to have this, you will have it. And I have to say, this industry really tests that. "How badly do you want it?" Because you've got to want it badly to do it. And that's one of the things I actually love about the industry: It doesn't put up with bullshit.

DV: Especially for appearing to be such a superficial industry.

TG: And you know, that is a matter of perception, and I loathe that perception because what we do really makes the world a more beautiful place . . . it makes people feel good about themselves. And whenever people say, "Oh, fashion's so ephemeral la-la-la-la," how do we really tell the history of our society and culture? When you look at it historically, it is through fashion . . . and that's not to be trivialized or discounted. It's really, really true. Furthermore, it's the semiology of dress. The clothes we wear send a message about how we want to be perceived. I don't believe many people are really aware of how profound that is, and I think if they were, they would think more thoughtfully about how they navigate the world.

DV: Thank you, Tim. I feel that only you would be able to express that message so effortlessly.

GREAT EXPECTATIONS

With trends changing faster than ever, an increased global influence, and the ability to purchase stylish pieces at virtually every price level (thanks in part to technology and fashion movers like retailers Zara and H&M), it's more apparent than ever that unique personal style is becoming increasingly accessible, even in seemingly secluded towns and cities. I remember being surprised that emo boys with shaggy hair and wearing eyeliner and skinny jeans weren't a rare sight at the local mall back home in Michigan, or that a suburban, straight guy-friend was not only well aware of who Karl Lagerfeld is and which high-end Parisian label he designs for but was also inspired by him and his fingerless-gloved ways! Through today's countless media outlets—television and film, award shows and fashion documentaries, music videos, the Internet, weekly magazines, celebrity coverage, and reality programming—fashion is brought to the forefront for not just the fashion elite but for everyone.

Uptown, downtown, and everywhere in between, New York offers literally thousands of stores and boutiques to choose from. Whether you're looking for name brands or no-name one-offs, the vast range of options offers shoppers and designers endless delight.

The increasing accessibility of virtually every category of style gives consumers more options than ever before—it's all literally at their fingertips. Images of Japanese punk street kids are easily a click away on the Web. What's hot in Milan or Paris is covered extensively in numerous, and now widely available, fashion magazines. When American designers such as Tom Ford and Thom Browne started offering Savile Row–level, custom-tailored suits, trips abroad for those services were no longer necessary. Not only is there a greater range of styles and designs for consumers to choose from, but the level of design is rising as well at every price point.

For a designer, establishing "brand loyalty"—branding oneself by establishing a target client, but without alienating too many others—can be a tricky thing in itself. This process goes far beyond offering the basics by giving clients a taste of the special world the designer has created just for them, whether with a sophisticated suit, a chic cocktail dress, or a killer bag. There are very specific reasons behind what people wear, be it a terrycloth sweat suit and a pair of Uggs or the skintight, décolletage-baring evening gown a young starlet dons for a red carpet event. There are choices made at every level of design, and it's the motivations behind those choices that will dictate whether a client will be back for more.

Simply walking the streets of New York is one of my favorite pastimes. The sidewalks teem with an endless array of natives and visitors alike, some of whom catch my eye with their presence and sense of style, and all of whom add their unique energy to the pulse of the city.

Who are your favorite designers?
Kris van Assche, Rag and Bone, Michael Bastian.

What is one of your favorite pieces of clothing and why?
The Coach shoulder bag my dad gave to me on the day I left for college. I love the way the leather is beginning to wear and darken in certain areas. It reminds me of my first baseball glove.

What draws you to a specific designer and why do you keep going back?
I'm drawn in by the way in which they reference the past. With the exception of the most cutting-edge or futuristic designers, most fashion operates on a certain sense of nostalgia. If I am interested in the visual nods to history a certain designer employs, then I am fascinated by the clothes and am curious what direction the designer will move to next.

If practicality wasn't an option, who would you wear everyday?
I would wear black jeans and a Hanes T-shirt everyday. Unfortunately, I have to pay the rent, which requires me to get dressed up sometimes.

Do you have an individual philosophy about your personal style?
I think both men and women look their best in black. It is a blank canvas in a way . . . a very New York blank canvas, but a blank canvas for a person's individuality to shine nonetheless.

Who is your style icon?
The entire cast of Michaelangelo Antonioni's L'Avventura for the entire film's beauty tinged with sadness; Paul Newman for his elegance and his understated manner of dress; Serge Gainsbourg for his love of life; and my dad, because he is the most interesting person I know.

Erik Rocca

ASSISTANT DIRECTOR
Edwynn Houk Gallery

Ellee Lee

ARCHITECT IN NYC

Who are your favorite designers?

Prada and Marni, Miu Miu, Marc Jacobs, 3.1 Philip Lim . . . too many!!

What is one of your favorite pieces of clothing and why?

My first Marni skirt—the first of anything is special, especially if it's Marni.

What draws you to a specific designer and why do you keep going back?

Some designers' clothes can really define you, even with a small piece. I am a visual person. I don't tell people who I am; I want people to recognize it.

If practicality wasn't an option, who would you wear everyday?

Prada? No, maybe Marc Jacobs! I know I'll always enjoy the morning then.

Do you have an individual philosophy about your personal style?

I don't really have a specific personal philosophy about my style. I just like to be comfortable with whatever I wear.

Who is your style icon?

I love the Olsen twins' style; it's experimental but not crazy. I also love Audrey Hepburn. She is simple but classy and charming as well; Audrey is always in style.

Syd Kato

WRITER

Who are your favorite designers?
Balenciaga—exquisite. Maison Martin Margiela—innovative. Equestrian Riding Apparel—timeless.

What is one of your favorite pieces of clothing and why?
Maison Martin Margiela broken-button trench coat from Spring/Summer '07: it's elegant, pulled, broken . . . and perfect.

What draws you to a specific designer and why do you keep going back?
Integrity and Quality . . . I like high IQ.

If practicality wasn't an option, who would you wear everyday?
My dog, Boris.

Do you have an individual philosophy about your personal style?
Style with a little wear and tear. Some of my favorite pieces of clothing are just like my favorite memories: so good, I can't let them go . . . they just keep getting more tattered and more favorite.

Who is your style icon?
Charlotte Gainsbourg—she's natural, genuine, and sweet.

Who are your favorite designers?

Well, I'm a big Marc Jacobs girl. Not only are his clothes beautiful but there is such amazing range and depth to his work. He's always playing with the idea of fashion and style and what it means to be "stylish." Daryl K has also always been a huge favorite of mine. Her clothes are punky and pretty—I still troll eBay for those amazing K-189 hoodies with the back pouch. From afar I definitely admire Alexander McQueen; from close up though I love H&M—they always have the best stuff!

What is one of your favorite pieces of clothing and why?

I actually have one of the big chunky sweaters from one of Marc's earliest collections for a company called Sketchbook—it even predates Perry Ellis. It's one of those pieces that is special and collectible—it represents a very specific time in the career of a designer that I love.

What draws you to a specific designer and why do you keep going back?

I think what draws anyone to a designer or label is "Can I wear this?" "Is this me?" But I think what keeps me coming back is when a designer continues to change and evolve while keeping his or her eye on that initial *je ne sais quoi* that attracted me in the first place. I like lots of options.

If practicality wasn't an option, who would you wear everyday?

Since practicality doesn't factor, I'm going to shoot for the moon and say Chanel Couture and, since a girl can't wear gowns all the time, probably the Gap for basics.

Do you have an individual philosophy about your personal style?

Not really. I tend to just wear what makes me feel good on a given day. I like the idea of playing dress up—anything from rock star to preppy and proper. My main goal is to just make sure I look at home in whatever I'm wearing.

Who is your style icon?

Of course I have to say my mother—she has great taste and, while we don't see eye-to-eye on everything, I know if she's not at least sixty percent with me on something then I'm probably wrong. At the risk of sounding trite, I'd also have to pick Jackie O.—I love anyone who radiates that kind of polish. Effortless glamour can be overrated.

Grainne Belluomo

ASSISTANT AT A COMEDY CLUB

Moonlights in the retail sciences.

LAUREN DAVID PEDEN

LAUREN DAVID PEDEN IS THE NEW YORK–BASED FASHION/ENTERTAINMENT JOURNALIST BEHIND THE FASHION INFORMER (WWW. THEFASHIONINFORMER.COM). Her articles have appeared in the *New York Times*, *UK Vogue.com*, *Time Out*, *Surface*, *ELLE*, *Allure*, *Glamour*, *Self*, *Travel + Leisure*, *In Style*, *TV Guide*, *Mademoiselle*, *Parade*, **and many other national publications.** A former contributing editor at *Fashion Wire Daily* and copywriter at *Vogue*, Lauren has also published seven books on various topics. Understanding a designer's point of view and personal vision is no small feat, but Lauren welcomes the opportunity to get into their creative minds; from her cozy West Village apartment she discussed how and why she does it.

DV: How did you come to be a fashion journalist? What steps did you take through your career and education to get here?

LDP: I grew up loving books and magazines—fashion magazines in particular. From the time I was eleven I was reading *Vogue* and *Harper's Bazaar*. I've always been intrigued by really good writing. I was besotted by the idea of fashion as possibility—of reinventing yourself—because I grew up in a small town in upstate New York, and I'd look at these fashion magazines and see not just the glamour of it . . . like, *Glamour* used to do the "back to college" thing, and I was eleven thinking, "Oh, my God! I'm going to go to college, and I could wear some Ralph Lauren toggle coat or some crazy thing . . ." It sort of gave me an idea, through clothes, to imagine the life I could have outside this very small town.

DV: What happened after you moved to New York?

LDP: I worked in retail in SoHo in the mid to late 1980s, when it was full of galleries and really cool, independent stores. I didn't get into publishing until I was 27, after I went back to school. I hadn't quite figured out what I wanted to do—I knew I wanted writing and knew I wanted fashion, but I wasn't sure how to merge the two. So I moved back in with my parents and put myself through school working three jobs. I graduated and interviewed with Condé Nast, and they said, "We really like you, but unfortunately we can't place you in editorial because you don't have a four-year degree." So I worked in

personnel for a year and became a Condé Nast rover, which means you're an in-house temp and you go wherever they tell you to go. So I was at *Vogue* for a month, and I was at *GQ* three to four months, and during that time, I happened to work with a great woman who let me write. And that's unheard of! From there I got hired in the articles department at *Mademoiselle*. I worked first as an editorial assistant and then as the research editor, which basically means I fact-checked every single article in *Mademoiselle* in 1989 and '90 by myself. Can you imagine?

DV: No, I can't!

LDP: It was a great training ground though, because it made me a good reporter. You learn how to ask questions. Now I have been a freelance writer for eighteen years. For the first three years I was fact-checking to pay the bills and getting as many writing assignments as I could, and slowly I started getting enough writing assignments that I could let the fact-checking go. I was still writing for *Mademoiselle*, and then I started writing for *Bride*, *American Health*, and *US* magazine before it went weekly. I started for the *New York Times* in 1993, and now I write for the *Styles* section.

DV: How did you veer into writing about fashion more exclusively?

LDP: I interviewed somebody at a gallery for a Christmas fashion story as a sidebar to a fashion piece I wrote for *Time Out* magazine. And about a year later I got an e-mail from a woman saying, "I'm going to be the managing editor of *Fashion Wire Daily*. We're looking for new writers; do you want to come in and meet?" So I did. And within a month of meeting her I was a contributing editor, and that's how I got into fashion full time. I realized I loved the pace of *FWD*. It was extremely liberating and I had a lot more autonomy. I would tell them what I wanted to write about; I would tell them whom I wanted to interview. I did the "Shopping With" column once a week for three years, which really let me hone my voice as a fashion writer and as a writer in general, because I went from writing maybe ten to twenty pieces per month for lots of different people to writing five to ten pieces a week for one publication, about one topic. So having been a Joe-of-all-trades, I do think there's something to be said for narrowing your focus.

DV: Would you recommend a similar path for young fashion journalists who are deciding where they want to work?

LDP: I would say it depends on the person. I would counsel them to try to find as many fashion writing assignments as they can. If they can't—work is work. Then you supplement. If somebody likes fashion but also music or travel or other types of design, I would say to do what you can, because that might help you narrow your focus. Everything builds on everything else. There is no "bad" experience when it comes to work, as far as I'm concerned. It all feeds into the next thing, and into your development as a creative person.

DV: Knowing that your words have power, do you feel a certain responsibility when writing about a designer's work?

LDP: Absolutely. In fact, I get very angry when I read journalists who do not seem to understand the power that their words and their opinions have. This was brought home to me in a very real way. When I first started at *Fashion Wire Daily*, I reviewed a designer's collection poorly, and he e-mailed me the next day and was definitely defensive, telling me point by point why I was wrong, and I don't think that's the right path to take. I forwarded it to his publicist and said, "I just want you to see what your client is doing here." But I realized maybe I was a little harsher in my delivery than I should have been. Whether I like a collection or not, a designer has put his heart and soul into it, and so I am careful to be critical of the work and not the designer, and to word my criticism in such a way that it's constructive—not criticism for the sake of being critical. It's the same thing that I look for with a good editor— as a writer, the best ones are those who help you to be better at what you do, who help take you to the next level. And I think a good critic can actually do that for a designer.

DV: Do you feel that the words of fashion critics and writers are as influential now as they have been throughout the past few decades?

LDP: Yes, I do. I think it's changing because of the Internet. I read and comment on [the *New York Times'*] Cathy Horyn's blog all the time. I think Cathy does a brilliant job. Robin Givhan, from the *Washington Post*, won a Pulitzer Prize, so she's got to be doing something right! I think *Vogue's* Sally Singer does a great job of disseminating the trends and putting them in a cultural context, which is a very tough thing to do. So I do think the opinions of certain people still have a lot of weight. And if that were not the case, critics wouldn't sometimes get banned from a designer's show.

DV: On fashion blogs, everyone can be a critic! What do you like about blogs?

LDP: For the most part, I like that blogs seem to attract a very passionate, articulate, intellectual person who not only views fashion but dissects it and looks at the backstory and has a historical perspective. And I like that you can go on and read not just what Cathy Horyn has to say about a collection, but also what thirty other people have to say—some are in the industry, some are totally removed from it, but they all bring something to the table. And it enhances your view of what you've seen. Sometimes it will make me go back and look at a collection with a different eye.

DV: Do you have a particular story that you either read or wrote that was very memorable?

LDP: I did a review of the Anne Klein/Isabel Toledo final show. The whole experience was moving, but I was also very pleased that I was able to articulate what I was trying to say. When I was growing up, Anne Klein meant something, and now it doesn't mean what it used to. And I had this moment, seeing those clothes come down the runway, of "Oh my God, [Isabel] is revitalizing a brand." I was crying. I thought, this is what Anne Klein is supposed to be, and it's different, and it's right for now, and it's bringing Isabel Toledo's taste level to a more mass audience. I think I was able to convey all of that in my review.

DV: Tell us about your website, *The Fashion Informer*.

LDP: I started it when I left *Fashion Wire Daily*. *The Fashion Informer* is my baby. I just started a column called "Meet Your Maker," and it's a behind-the-scenes look at a particular designer: I did one with Tom Scott, a knitwear designer, and one with Gaby, from Tucker by Gaby Basora. Yeohlee Teng is coming up. I like taking readers into the process and talking to a designer not just about a collection but how they work and how they get from A to Z. On the site I also do "Random Questions For . . ." where I ask designers and fashion editors things like, "What did you have for breakfast this morning?" "What's in current rotation on your iPod?" It offers a more personal perspective on people. And that's one of the things I like about writing in general—hopefully conveying the essence of the person I'm profiling accurately, with respect, but also in a way that brings something different to light about them that the public might not know. My favorite thing is when I get a note from somebody after a piece has come out, saying, "I just want to thank you. You got me. Your story meant so much to me because I feel like you're the first journalist who's really understood who I am, and it was such a great read." Honestly, it sounds kind of corny, but I really feel privileged when people entrust me to tell their stories.

SUCCESSFUL SILHOUETTES

I'd now like to venture into some specifics about design in order to guide you through the daunting task of dressing not only yourself but someone else. I'd like to begin by using my lovely friend Anna as a model. She was gracious—and brave—enough to bare all in a leotard just for us. We're going to begin by looking at her—and I mean *really* looking at her: her shape, her proportions, her skin color, her size, her hair, and her assets (especially the ones she wants to deemphasize). During this meeting, Anna confessed that, as a rule, she likes to showcase only one area of her body at a time, whether it's her legs, her chest, her back, etc., but too much at once can easily go too far. Paying special attention to Anna's shape, I'm really immediately drawn to her amazingly long legs, as well as her slender neck, and really want to focus my design emphasis on these features. Her rib cage and bust are proportionately a bit smaller, so my first reaction is to add some fullness to the top half of her body, which could also be achieved through a visual distraction with a contrasting color or pattern.

As a budding accessory designer herself, my dear Anna is quite familiar with the design process and how in-depth it can become, especially when working one-on-one with a client. Her requirements for her party dress were simple: Chic. Special. Fun. *That* I can do. We first talked color choices, and based on her fair skin, blonde hair, and blue eyes (which means she can wear pretty much any color) we opted to delve into the green family, something that was saturated, but still light in hue, and we ended up with an intriguing yellow-green chartreuse color, more specifically labeled by my handy Pantone book as #16-0532. (Personally, I like "yellow-green chartreuse color" better.) I also wanted to bring a metallic somewhere into the outfit for two main reasons: First, I thought that it would play unexpectedly, yet beautifully, off the green fabric, and second, because I was designing a party dress, and if that doesn't give me an excuse to add some shine then I don't know what does!

Designing to a particular woman's shape is obviously an important consideration, but not being dictated to solely by the "rules" of fashion is at times what makes an even stronger statement. Imagine if every designer stuck to the same rules that have been around for years: Women would still be wearing restricting corsets and hoop skirts every day, taping down their chests for an appropriate 1920s-era flapper look, or not even having the option of wearing pants! Even in modern times, rules and design tips are constantly being rehashed in practically every style guide or design textbook out there; the world would be a very boring place if we all stuck with little black dresses and pointy black shoes. Granted, the mantras "black is slimming," "pearls are elegant," and "jeans are comfortable" are great guidelines for most people, but if designers never thought outside of convention and beyond what already exists today, style would never move forward.

This leads me back to Anna and the design I created for her. Although she wasn't too specific in the particulars of her birthday design (and I didn't ask her to be—ha ha!), she told me that she desired something bold, creative, and unlike anything she already had hanging in her closet. This is particularly why I opted for the untraditional cocoon silhouette for her. It showcases her long legs (and, as she said, nice backside) while the metallic silver and ombré piecing near the neckline creates interest and visual "weight" on her proportionally smaller shoulder frame. I was ultimately aiming to balance her shape a bit, while still maintaining the chic, modern look that would please us both. Many other silhouettes would work well on Anna's slender frame, although an A-line dress design consisting of spaghetti straps, a fitted torso, and molded bra cups would only draw more attention to her narrow torso and small bust. These same elements, however, would look amazing on a woman with fuller hips and chest. By raising the hemline of Anna's dress, it created a path for the eyes to move up, up, up her body. If I had made the dress longer, but still slim, a similar effect would have happened, but the blatantly fun sex appeal would have been lost. Check out the end result on page 90.

Check out the end result on page 90.

Understanding how shape and form affect the body is an elemental part of designing clothing. When developing silhouettes, it's important to think three-dimensionally, as this is ultimately how the garment will appear. Keeping in mind not only the integrity of the garment but also the customer will help the work come together more cohesively. A fashion-forward customer may prefer avant-garde shapes and progressive designs, while a more traditional woman may prefer safer, more subdued silhouettes that are slightly altered and updated.

STRIVING FOR INNOVATION

Standing out in the fashion world is almost always a good thing. In an industry that's only too happy to boast the discovery of the next "it" designer/dress/bag, it can be quite an uphill battle to get to the top. No, scratch that: It can be tough as hell just to make it down the rubble-strewn path that leads to the bridge that leads to the hidden trail that leads to the base of the hill! For every "next big thing" there are literally hundreds of designers who have come and gone or whose designs will never make it onto someone's back. Although the reasons that one designer succeeds and another fails are too numerous to list, striving for an original voice and distinctive point of view is one of the best ways for a designer to improve his or her odds for exposure and success. Throughout fashion history, fearless designers have created and defined new looks and images, whether introducing new silhouettes, distinctive attitudes, or unique perspectives that are decidedly their own. Some designers have made names for themselves by reinterpreting (or, it could be argued, replicating) the work of other designers, but only those who have produced unique, original work truly stand out. Christian Dior, Cristóbal Balenciaga, and Alexander McQueen are a few designers whom I greatly admire and who have forged exciting new paths that countless others have followed.

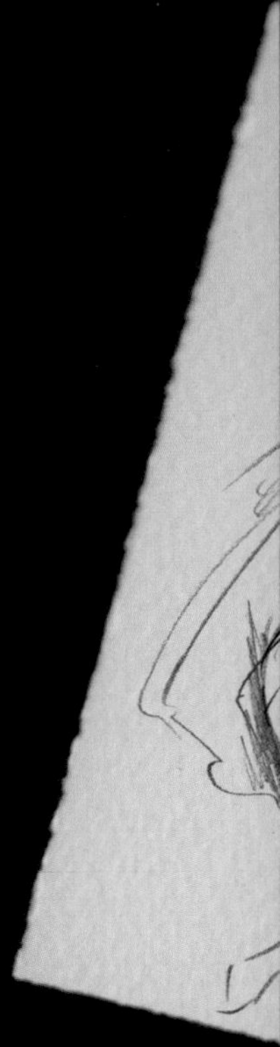

Dior's "New Look," for example, was a direct response to the restrictions of minimal postwar fashion, which consisted of handmade, sharp-shouldered suits and knee-length skirts that were the necessary result of years of supply rationing and public restraint and modesty. The New Look debuted in spring 1947 and featured soft shoulders, waspy waists, and full skirts (seen in my sketch at left) reminiscent of the romantic belle epoque ideal that was so popular in the early 1900s. After the years of intense hardship brought on by World War II, people became excited about fashion again, in part spurred on by the optimism and forward thinking that the New Look represented.

Balenciaga's manipulation of shape and form also made him a standout in the fashion world in the 1950s and '60s. His unique silhouettes are still acknowledged as innovative: His famed square coat, high-waisted babydoll dress, gracefully draped cocoon coat, sack dress, and balloon jacket and skirt (made in two versions, both as a single pouf and doubled with one pouf on top of the other, as seen at left) are just a few examples of his original and distinctively modern style. Although Balenciaga's fluid, organic shapes differed greatly from Dior's widely popular New Look, it was this contrast that helped keep him in the spotlight.

Alexander McQueen is an example of a contemporary designer who strives continuously for innovation not only in his designs but in their presentation (as this photograph attests). Since the mid 1990s, some of McQueen's most memorable runway shows have featured a live model being spray-painted by robots, a huge chessboard, wolves, a dance extravaganza, and headdresses adorned with stuffed birds in flight. Theatrics aside, his clothing stands on its own, an absolute wonderment of superb construction and exquisite detail. His outlandish presentations and uncensored comments may make headlines, but it's his well-thought-out, fashion-forward designs, like his modern take on Savile Row–quality tailored garments, that make him a successful designer.

Though not every designer will be the next Dior, Balenciaga, or McQueen—or even wants to be, for that matter—striving for innovation will only push their designs forward. Even if that push is at a much slower pace, with minimal steps forward—say, at a moderate-level, corporate design company where change doesn't come as quickly—it still must move forward or it will become stagnant. For example, designers at both Dior and the Gap may be asked to sketch out fifty new sweater designs for the upcoming fall season, but since the client profile is extensively broader at the Gap, their options will be more muted and relatable, whereas Dior has a much more specific customer; both brands have customers with definitive needs, profiles, and expectations, but the final product could not be more different. To be a good designer, it's imperative to understand the market you are designing in and to bring as many new ideas and fresh concepts as possible to the targeted market, whether that's cotton twin sets or bias-cut silk gowns.

NINA GARCIA

NINA GARCIA IS MOST PUBLICLY KNOWN FOR HER ROLE as the incredibly astute, high-heeled judge and critic who pulls no punches on the Emmy-nominated series *Project Runway*. As the former fashion director of *ELLE* magazine, she worked closely with top designers and stylists and pinpointed the trends of the season in her monthly mission to develop the ultimate look book and shopping guide for stylish women around the globe. Nina is no stranger to change, having seen countless fashions come and go during her career. It was great to hear firsthand about a few of her personal favorites and what she continually looks for in young designers.

"

DV: For the pages of *ELLE*, where do you look for inspiration?

NG: Oh, we find inspiration from everywhere! It can be a film, a piece of art. It could be anything. It could be *someone*. It could be a girl walking down the street. It just could be anything that could inspire us.

DV: Wow!

NG: I think that was one of the most incredible and educational moments for me because I wasn't alive back then to see these things—this was before my time as an editor—and to be there and to be able to see that was *the* moment. That was one of my most memorable fashion moments and inspiring and just . . . everything.

DV: What to you defines the difference between fashion and clothing?

NG: It's really when you move the design process, you know? There are certainly a lot of clothes, but maybe the inspiring fashion moment is when you're really moving that design process forward. When you see something that really is . . . just, like, "Wow, I've never seen that interpretation." Or, "That's a very interesting way." I'm not saying weird, different . . .

DV: Unique.

NG: It is unique and it's moving the design process forward. It's just something you never thought about and, "Oh, what an interesting way to do that." That's, I think, the difference.

DV: You've been quoted before as saying that you are a big supporter of young designers, but what is it about young designers that excites you, and specifically, why did you join *Project Runway*? What is it about that raw talent?

NG: Seeing something unique, seeing something different, seeing a point of view—I see that in the show all the time. You have to have a point of view. Yes, you have to change with the seasons and keep things moving, but I'm always encouraging a designer to have a point of view or something that defines them, so that when I see a garment, I'm like, "Oh yes, that is Daniel Vosovic."

DV: Regardless of the season or the trend.

NG: Exactly. That has *your* mark on it. Also finding something unique, a fresh perspective, and something that sets them apart from the rest. I don't really want to see another new designer copying somebody else or rehashing something that has already been done. Yes, I think we all can be inspired by Poiret or by Saint Laurent, but at the end of the day I do want to see something unique. I want to see something personal. I want to see something that is *theirs*.

DV: Absolutely, because I think a lot of young designers feel the need to chase the trends—to do what the "big guys" are doing. But when it's already being documented, it's already too late.

NG: Right. Be yourself.

DV: Do you have any advice or guidelines for young designers who are looking to get their work seen by the right people? Do you have any ideas, besides being on a reality TV show, of course? How does everyone else do it?

NG: They call. They have a lot of perseverance. They put together look books. They send you pictures or full packages of their work. Some will go the retail route if they're lucky. It kind of works either way, and I try to help in that way, too; if there's somebody new that is interesting to me that I have seen, I will pass him or her along to a retailer—I will speak to my contacts from Bergdorf's and I'll say, "I saw somebody really interesting." And the same goes for them. I will talk to them and I'll be like, "Have you seen anybody? Have you uncovered anybody that is interesting?" And part of what we do as editors is try to look for *those* people, to hear if there's somebody out there in Brooklyn, or sitting in their showroom working away—we are seeking out *that* person, so we are receptive to receiving pictures or hearing about it.

DV: Do you get just about *everyone* then, trying to get a meeting?

NG: Well, I also think there're a lot of people who think, "Well I'm just going to sew this up and present it and see," and that all of a sudden there's going to be a career. There needs to be a little more than that. There needs to be maybe a little bit of a business plan to back it up. It's not just, "I'm going to go into your house and see your new dresses"—it just doesn't work like that. Because it needs to be a little more professional and a little more serious.

DV: I was talking with a patternmaker who has worked for everyone from Wal-Mart to Oscar de la Renta, but she's also an instructor, and she was saying, "The biggest advice I have for young designers now is to have a business sense, because you have to have more than just pretty clothes."

NG: Right.

DV: And you have to have the ability to produce those and you have to have the ability to market yourself. And a lot of people think that once you have a fashion show, that's the exclamation point.

NG: No. That is not . . . that's a beginning.

DV: Absolutely.

NG: So it takes more now than that—maybe that's what worked twenty years ago, but no, there are more elements to it. You need to be business savvy. You need to have a personality where you can market yourself. You need to also be creative . . . so it takes a lot to be a designer now.

DV: Exactly, and how fast things go nowadays just makes it even more difficult to keep up.

NG: And it's a serious problem—it has always been fast, but now the stakes are even higher. It's an even bigger industry that moves a lot of money.

DV: There is no cookie-cutter method for making it.

NG: No, not anymore, because what worked for Carolina Herrera and what worked for Oscar de la Renta and what worked for Calvin Klein is not necessarily going to work now. Those were other times. It was a very different competition. It was a very different arena they were playing in.

DV: Especially with the progression of technology and today's advancements in transporting images around the world in a matter of seconds.

NG: You can see shows in less than five minutes at the same time we're seeing them in Milan or Paris—the luxury business has also changed considerably. I think it's going to keep changing. So there are no rules.

DV: Do you have anything else you'd like to touch upon?

NG: I want to impress to just think out of the box. Maybe it's the most unexpected thing—do the most unexpected thing, just don't do the expected. I think the best idea is just to do what *you* think. There are no right and wrong rules anymore.

DV: Young designers will love to hear that! That's more important than you think, because coming from you, that has a lot of impact.

NG: Well, it's like looking back through fashion; I think if you look at the history of fashion and the history of things that do well, most are things that—

DV: Have woken people up and surprised people at that time.

NG: Yes, they surprised. I think that what has happened with this generation is that we are too comfortable kind of repeating, and going through the circles, and going back to the trends and going back to all of the same things, and we need people to break the rules, break ground, and be the innovators. That's what we are missing most of. So break the rules and think outside of the box. Surprise us all, because those are the people that are going to seize the season. Those are going to be the next Calvins, the next Ralphs . . .

DV: The next Nicolas Ghesquière [at Balenciaga]!

NG: Yes, well, there you go.

DV: If he's not a rule breaker, I don't know who is.

NG: Exactly.

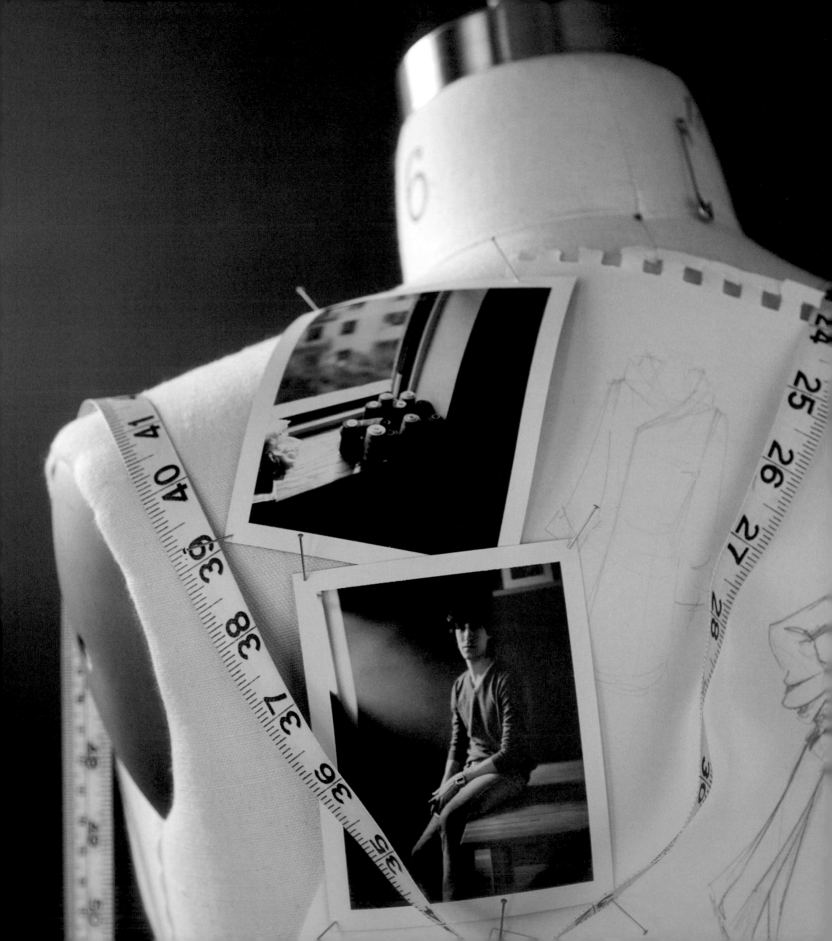

THE
EXECUTION

CREATING A GARMENT

IN ARCHITECTURE, THE BASE ON WHICH A STRUCTURE IS BUILT DETER-MINES ITS STRENGTH, STYLE, AND LONGEVITY. The same is true in fashion: The pattern from which a garment is constructed is perhaps the most crucial element of the design process. Details not only make the difference, but they ultimately define the quality of a garment, and it all starts with the foundation, so to speak. A great pattern is truly a work of art, and its subtleties can determine whether the resulting garment looks and feels like a custom fit or something you bought off a shady street vendor.

THE BIG
RUB-OFF

There is one exception to creating an original pattern for a garment, a dirty little secret of prêt-à-porter (ready-to-wear) fashion that has, for the most part, been kept relatively under wraps to those not in the know—until now, that is. (Man, I hope I'm not ripped apart for letting this one out.) Of course, every industry has its shortcuts, but in fashion there's one in particular that almost everyone has used at one point or another, and it's called a *rub-off.* A rub-off consists of taking an existing garment, "rubbing off" the seam lines, design features, and overall shape onto paper, and thus creating a pattern without starting from a blank slate.

The following tools are necessary to complete a rub-off: pattern paper, clear ruler, pencil, paper scissors, pins, and, of course, the garment you wish to rub off.

Home sewers have used rub-offs for years to replicate their favorite designer looks, and I've been in numerous fashion design studios where a competitor's jacket or "bestselling pant" hangs in the closet either cut apart or covered with pins and chalk markings galore. Professional designers use rub-offs beçause they accelerate the design process, thus lowering the cost of creating the final product; simply put, time that isn't spent on the trial and error of creating a pattern from scratch means money that's saved on development and sewing. In addition to wanting to share some insider knowledge, my main purpose in sharing this information is to provide a learning tool for beginning and aspiring designers, as a guide to how the best have done it—fashion *CliffsNotes*, so to speak. I guess the old saying that imitation is the sincerest form of flattery could be used most appropriately here.

Again, I repeat, the reasoning behind my including this section is to show a template for how others have done it before but also to impress the importance of not stopping at a direct copy, as that is not designing. I compare it to reading a great novel before setting out to write one of your own; although this is a great way to learn and understand the process, one would never think to label the original one's own. Furthermore, at the time I'm writing this book, fashion designs and patterns are not eligible for copyright protection, which thus makes the business of counterfeiting a very frustrating gray area. Although designers can become known for often designing in a certain silhouette, color, or fit (Dior's 1940s iconic shape, Valentino's red, Proenza Schouler's seamed bra cup bustier), it's often difficult to determine an original design from a replication, unless it is an obvious and blatant copy. Unfortunately, this happens all the time, traditionally with moderate or mass-market stores selling watered-down versions of what designers showed most recently on their runways. A few well-established designers have battled the copycats in court, but when considering the high cost of lawyers and litigation fees, a designer must weigh the benefits in each situation carefully.

I've recruited patternmaker extraordinaire Laura Moore to tackle the task of rubbing off a button-down shirt from a local retailer. With more than twenty years of experience in the industry, and having worked for an array of clients ranging from Wal-Mart to Oscar de la Renta, this woman knows her stuff (see my interview with Laura on page 78). So get your pencils, pins, and paper ready for a crash course in how to do a rub-off. What follows are the basic steps accompanied at right by a visual overview of the process.

Rub-Off Instructions: Button-Up Shirt With Darts

Body

1. Mark the grain line on pattern paper—this shows which way the fabric goes.
2. Reposition the garment as many times as necessary until the grain line of the garment matches the grain line on pattern paper.
3. Begin with the main body parts—the front and back body panels—working from largest to smallest. Place the garment on center front and center back.
4. Pin the garment along seam lines.
5. For dart pick-up, pin around seam lines until you get to the legs of the dart (the portion of the dart where two points come together). Reposition the garment so side seam is flat and then re-pin dart. This is your dart pick-up.
6. Inspect your garment. Does it have a folded placket or a separate placket? Feel for seam allowance (the area between the fabric edge and the stitching line). Mark your buttons and buttonholes. *(Knits usually have ³⁄₈" or ¹⁄₄" seam allowance. Wovens usually have ¹⁄₂" or ⁵⁄₈" seam allowance. Collars/necklines/outward seams usually have ¹⁄₄" or ³⁄₈" seam allowance.)*
7. True, or mark in, the lines of a two-part collar separately.

Sleeve

1. Front and back armholes must be rubbed off separately, as front cap and back caps are usually different. Thread trace (trace with long stitches with a needle and thread) the back sleeve cap and front sleeve cap in order to see the difference.
2. Work with the grain line on folded paper.
3. Place the back side of the sleeve up, as it's the more complicated side.
4. Mark the edge of sleeve where it pulls away from the paper edge; this is your pleat pick-up.
5. True all the seams.
6. True each piece the same way for all pattern drafts.
7. Rub off all pieces of the garment before truing and finalizing each pattern piece.

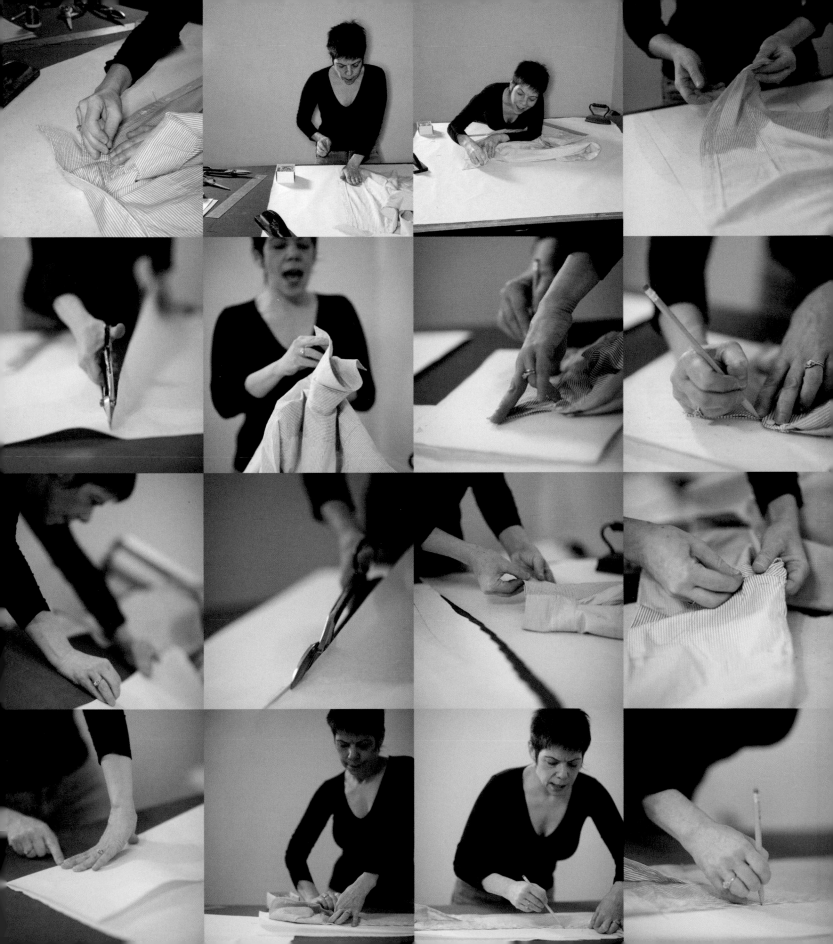

Rub-Off Instructions: T-Shirt

For the most part, T-shirts have an almost identical rub-off for the body as a woven shirt does. Work with the T-shirt inside out, as it's easier to match seams that way. Also, knit patterns should be used only for knit fabrics that have similar stretch, give, and weight.

1. **Pin two layers of folded paper together; both should have a center front grain line fold.**
2. **Square a line across for the bottom of the shirt. Add the hem according to the seam allowance on the shirt.**
3. **Pencil in front and back necklines at the same time (not the rib).**
4. **Add all seam allowances and then cut out. (*Traditional shoulder seam for a T-shirt is ¼" forward. Add ¾" seam allowance for hem and ⅜" seam allowance for all other seams.*)**
5. **Pin the shoulders together. Check for a smooth transition at the neck.**
6. **To make the rib lay flat, measure the inside of the neck (edge of seam allowance, not the actual seam line) to find correct length.**
7. **Always label each of your pattern pieces with style number/name, piece name, number of pieces to cut, and size. Place all pieces into an envelope and put a cutter's must (an itemized list of the pattern piece components) on the outside of the envelope.**

So now that there is an established paper pattern to work with, don't be afraid to jump in and start changing elements to make it yours: lengthening, cropping, or widening the sleeves, designing a different collar, or manipulating a dart are all great places to begin. A designer new to patternmaking and rub-offs may also consider combining elements from existing commercial patterns—a sleeve, collar, or lapel, for example—to help gain confidence in his or her skills before attempting to design solely from the ground up. Granted, the pattern may end up looking a bit like the patchwork of Frankenstein, but until the knowledge is there it's okay to look to how others have done it before.

When I spoke with the ingenious Todd Oldham, creator of everything from gorgeous one-of-a-kind gowns to streamlined La-Z-Boy sofas, about sources of inspiration, he talked about the two ways that he learned about sportswear: being broke as a kid and shopping at the Salvation Army, and working in the alterations department at the Dallas Ralph Lauren. He considers the Salvation Army to be comparable to "a couture salon filled with one-offs, incredible things made way better than what I could afford." Todd spent his time scouring their racks for garments that he could rip apart and sew back together again so that he could understand the intricacies of how each was made. Also in his youth, he worked in the sweltering back room of a Ralph Lauren alterations department, continuing to hone his eye and learning things rarely covered in a textbook or classroom (see Todd's interview on page 10).

"LAURA MOORE

LAURA MOORE IS AN ADJUNCT ASSOCIATE PROFESSOR IN THE FASHION DEPARTMENT AT PRATT INSTITUTE. She balances her education career with freelance patternmaking and consulting for fashion startups out of her New York studio. Her own work runs the gamut from vintage-inspired hand tailoring to soft-circuit wiring and electronic "wearables." Getting to know Laura has been a particularly satisfying experience for me; I admire her extensive knowledge of patterns and problem-solving skills, but also the mentoring position she has innately grown into as an educator to the next generation of designers.

DV: Could you please start by letting us know how you got here? Did you have any formal training or are you primarily self-taught?

LM: I am pretty much self-taught. When I was really little I made clothes for my stuffed animals out of aluminum foil, paper towels. I learned how to knit on toothpicks.

DV: Excellent!

LM: I spent my childhood selling, knitting, crocheting, generally being pretty grandmotherly and not so much a normal kid. I made wild Halloween costumes. It never occurred to me that I could pursue this as a career. I was in college, an ancient languages major, whipping up a dress in the lounge in my dorm in my spare time, and a girl who lived on my floor basically said, "You know, Laura, you're an idiot. You have this talent . . . what are you doing?" So I did a year at FIT, was bored, went back and got an academic degree in psychology. I've been in the industry since 1979. I have worked as a sample maker, a patternmaker, production manager, technical designer . . .

DV: You've worked with clients ranging from Wal-Mart to Oscar de la Renta, correct?

LM: Yes, that's correct. I have worked in menswear, swimwear, activewear. I did a little bit of bridal.

DV: Being a freelance patternmaker of sorts, could you shed some light on how the process happens with designers, and getting the work from one hand to the next?

LM: Well, the reality is that, these days, people like me get completely bypassed. Designers work with overseas vendors, and measurements, swatches, and increasingly the patterns are made at the factory level overseas.

DV: Both the hard-paper development patterns and the digital work? Are hard-paper patterns still relevant in today's digital world?

LM: Oh, yes! As a matter of fact, I'm packing up a box of fully graded, hard-paper patterns that are going to India, where they are going to be hand cut with large scissors, and they press the garments with a cold iron.

DV: So would you agree that though it's important to know the faster, easier way to do patterns and drawing, it's crucial to know how to do it by hand?

LM: Yes. We at Pratt are really moving into the computer age in terms of drawing, because our students need it for their portfolios and because positions as CAD artists are very plentiful. They're doing a lot of things digitally. One of the reasons I love teaching at Pratt is that we are an art school—we're not a trade school. And we teach our students draping and patternmaking the old-fashioned way. I teach a hand-tailoring class. My students learn techniques that have been in use for hundreds of years. They may never make another hand-tailored garment, but they understand the inner workings of construction so much better as a result.

DV: As a designer, I know how important it is to start with a great pattern as a good base, but what are some common misconceptions of young designers or even the consumer?

LM: What most people as consumers don't understand is that a size 6 is not a size 6 is not a size 6. Every company's size 6 may be a little bit different, and even if a designer sends the same tech pack with the same specifications to different overseas factories, there are different patternmakers with different styles in each of these factories. And the garments will be, for all intents and purposes, the same—they'll be to spec. But one pair of jeans is going to make you look like you have a tight ass and the other one is going to make you look a little wide-assed. They're very, very subtle differences. In fact, a lot of my private clients came to me because they sent garments to be copied overseas and they got things back that were recognizable as the same style but didn't fit right at all.

DV: Being a small-business owner as well as a professor, do you have any advice or words of wisdom for young designers?

LM: I tend not to encourage young designers to start a business if they're not really interested in business. One can be much more creative as a designer on staff for a company than as the owner of a small business, when you need to worry your pretty little head day in and day out about shipping and deliveries and office supplies and employees and customers who haven't paid you. I get a lot of inquiries from wannabe startups who have a "few sketches," new moms who think they can design better baby clothes, people who are outraged at the price of a designer wedding gown, etc. Or they assume that they can do better and make lots of money, and then I suggest to them that with all my years of expertise, I have never wanted to manufacture and sell designs.

DV: Anything else to share with the young minds of the world?

LM: I think it's a really important when you're young to learn everything you can. Test the waters. Think outside the box a little. Most of our fashion students want to do eveningwear or sportswear, and the reality of life is, the market for plus size, petite, maternity, sleepwear, children's wear—these markets are huge, and they may be a little less competitive. I've noticed that one student who may show a children's line as his or her senior thesis collection gets a job in children's wear, whereas the many who are showing sportswear or eveningwear are less likely to stand out.

DV: Is there anything you can think of from the academic standpoint?

LM: Well, I'm amazed about two things about my students: The first is that they don't look at clothes, not in the sense of turning them inside out and seeing how they go together, seeing what kind of fabrics are used as linings and interlinings. There is so much that one can learn on one's own. There's so much that is common sense. And while, as designers, we always want to come up with something unique and new, there are a lot of good, solid foundations without which it's just a pretty picture. This is the other thing that surprises me about my students: I taught very early on in my career and then didn't teach again until about twenty years later; it used to be that students would come to fashion school wearing their own designs, having sewn since childhood. Now they come in—they can draw pretty pictures and they love to shop. But many of them have never met a sewing machine. We have a generation that has grown up without Home Ec classes. We actually have two generations here, which means that today's youth are growing up without moms who sew and grandmas who maybe live in Florida. And it boggles my mind that people want to be fashion designers and it never occurred to them to make a garment.

DV: So, whether Grandma is around or not, learn the foundations!

LM: Yes, learn the foundations.

HANDS-ON DRAPING

So now that you know how a pattern can be made from an existing garment, let's look at a technique that's a bit more freestyle. **Draping fabric on a dress form allows a designer to work three-dimensionally and can be a much more organic, artistic process than sketching. The fashion industry is, of course, a time-pressured one, so draping tends to be the less-favored method for producing ready-to-wear collections because of the amount of time required for development and execution, not just of the garments themselves but of their details, which can be explored more quickly in a sketch.**

When designers use draping as a design tool, they begin by working out an idea on a dress form in order to translate it into something physical and then transfer it to a paper pattern to correct and balance the fit. This process can be seen on *Project Runway*, where draping allows the contestants to develop ambiguous ideas into gorgeous, one-of-a-kind creations. Due to the extreme time constraints on the show—we really do only have eight hours to sew a dress!—as well as the "no outside patterns" rule, draping is really the only option during the challenges. In a traditional studio setting, a design may be draped from conception, or adapted from an existing pattern, with sometimes as many as five samples being produced and revised throughout the process. On *Project Runway*, of course, it's crucial for designers to edit as they work, because there's literally no time (or even fabric) left for changes.

Designers who are new to draping should keep in mind that certain guidelines need to be followed, such as making sure that the grain of the fabric isn't at odds with the garment's construction and that there's a way to actually get *into* it—it can't just be pinned to the mannequin. Once those bases are covered, experimentation can begin! But if you're working with a gorgeous, $50-per-yard, hand-painted silk chiffon, the last thing you want to do is slash into it on a whim. A cost-efficient and productive way to work through the design process is to create a *muslin* first. A muslin is a test garment that's created in a fabric with a similar weight and hand (meaning dry, slippery, soft, rough, etc.) to the actual fabric before progressing to the final style. Muslin is also the term used for an inexpensive, unbleached cotton fabric that's commonly used for

A designer should always have a healthy supply of straight pins and muslin lying around, as one never knows when creative inspiration will hit. A snooty former professor of mine once told me that a professional designer never uses pins with the colored balls at the heads. Regardless of my distaste for his approach, I have to agree—it's best to let the design stand out, not the pins!

draping; it comes in a variety of weights, which should match that of the final fabric. If you have a difficult time imagining what the final garment will look like in something other than boring, itchy muslin, pick up a cheaper, synthetic version of the intended fabric as well and sew up another version to fit and test with.

Draping is still one of my favorite ways to design; it's much more exciting to me than either just sketching or making flat patterns. I actually find draping therapeutic, and the freedom of being able to just grab a few yards of fabric from my stock yardage and go to work gives me an extra burst of needed creative energy. Most designers tend to gravitate toward sketching or draping; personal preference is something that can only be determined by trying both. For those who both sketch and drape, it's up to the individual designer as to which happens first. I like to sketch out rough ideas before I bring fabric to the form, as creating loose boundaries for myself allows me to release my creativity through the design process. I'll usually start with a general shape or silhouette and then begin draping, with the smaller details becoming more defined as I work. I turn back to sketching as I think of refinements and then go back to the form again to see how they might evolve.

The process of designing my collection was also a hybrid of sketching and draping. I knew generally what I wanted to create for my client, Anna, and she wanted to see what I had planned, so initial sketches were beneficial to us both, especially before purchasing fabric. As the designs evolved on the dress form, I was able to adapt them to better suit her body: I brought in the shoulder width to balance her small frame, exaggerated the fullness in the waist to give her the drama she wanted, and chose fabrics whose colors I had envisioned as part of the collection but in shades that also beautifully complemented her features.

Draping: General Guidelines and Tips

- **Muslin comes in a variety of weights; choose the version that is most similar to the selected fabric. This will help ensure that the muslin pattern transfers correctly to the final garment.**

- **Muslin can become twisted on the roll, or from cutting or ripping it too aggressively, so before placing muslin on the dress form, it is sometimes necessary to "block" it, or realign the grain line by pulling opposing corners of the muslin (use a ruler to ensure that the grain line is straight). This is important because if a muslin is created off-grain, the following steps will be affected and result in a poorly made garment.**

- **When pinning, be sure to insert pins at an angle—not straight in at 90 degrees—to ensure that they don't fall or lift out easily.**

- **When draping a jacket or coat, don't forget to place the necessary inner construction elements such as shoulder pads on the dress form before draping, as they surely will dictate how the garment will fit and fall.**

- **Traditionally, notches on back pieces are indicated with a double slash, while front notches are done with a single slash. This will further help in keeping pattern pieces in order when they are taken off the form.**

- **Always be sure to use a light hand when draping. It's very easy to see when a muslin has been overworked: it is not only visually unappealing, but if the muslin is too distorted from aggressive pulling and excessive iron steaming, it must be redone, as it will never look the same in real fabric given all the manipulation.**

- **When creating a symmetrical design, such as a standard shirt or jacket, it is only necessary to drape half of it. Once the muslin is complete and transferred to a paper pattern, be sure to place the appropriate piece on the folded edge of the final fabric, thus cutting a balanced and symmetrical pattern.**

- **Have the design sketch close at hand for reference. Straight pins, scissors, tape measure, style tape, pencil, and muslin should also be readily available.**

BLE SHOULDER

6

SHOULDER

Step-by-Step Process

1. According to the design, first create the style lines by placing style tape on the dress form. Reposition the tape as many times as needed until you are satisfied and pin into place, if necessary *(figs. 01-02)*.

2. Work on one section at a time, usually beginning with the center front panel. Measure height and width of that section (i.e., front, bust panel, etc.), adding extra length and width for corrections and adjustments (I suggest at least 2" on all edges). Measure out appropriately sized muslin panel to begin draping *(fig. 03)*.

3. Pay attention to grain line as you position the muslin. Begin by pinning the middle top of the panel to secure it. Next, work your way down the panel, pinning as you go, and then out toward the edge. Confirm that there are no ripples, pulling, or gaping anywhere *(figs. 04-07)*.

4. Once you are satisfied with each section, take a sharp pencil and mark in style lines. Use your fingernail to help you find the seams on the dress form. Mark lines clearly with small, short dashes. Mark intersecting seam lines with a "+" (where the waist and side seam meet, for example) *(figs. 08-09)*.

5. Be sure to mark all relevant points, such as the bust apex, center front and center back, side seams, shoulder seam, armhole, hipline, neckline, etc. The more information the better, as it will help when replacing the muslin back on the form. Trim excess fabric, leaving ample seam allowance *(figs. 10-11)*.

6. It's important to look at the design as a whole, and not just section by section. I recommend taking a few steps back from the form every 15 minutes or so to get a full perspective. Also be sure to walk around the form to ensure it looks good from all angles *(fig. 12)*.

7. Continue working through the design, section by section, being sure to place notches on both pieces of shared seams, to help correctly piece everything together once it is all removed from the dress form *(figs. 13-16)*.

8. Once all sections have a finished muslin piece that is fully notched and labeled, take them all off the dress form and pin them together on a table. Be sure to fold/pin seam allowance to the inside, in order to see how the design will actually lay and fit. It's sometimes necessary to baste stitch (long, wide-set stitches that are easily removed) the muslin together to see how it will truly look; this is often the case with more complicated designs with multiple pattern pieces.

9. Use a contrasting pencil to mark corrections in balance and fit: I use blue for first corrections and red for second. This keeps my muslins from looking too overworked with pencil lines and ensures I transfer the correct notches.

10. Once a final muslin is approved, it can then be transferred to a paper pattern by tracing the corrected notches and seams with a tracing wheel and carbon paper. If the pattern pieces are slightly off or two notches don't match up, this is where they will need to be corrected and re-marked.

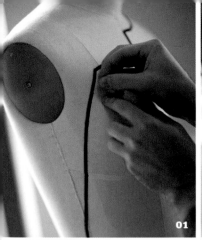

01

04

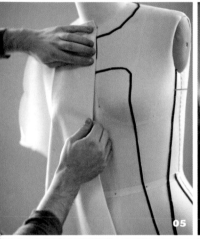

05

06

07

08

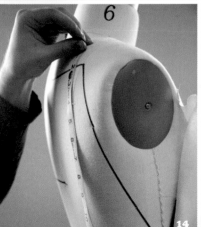

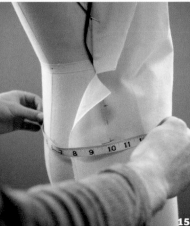

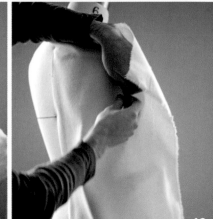

From Muslin to Paper Pattern

Once a draped design is complete, it's transferred to a paper pattern to be balanced and corrected, with all notches aligned and seam lines matched. Here are the basic steps:

1. Confirm that the finished muslin is properly pinned and marked *before* taking it off the dress form.

2. Once the muslin is on the table, double-check that all notches are clearly marked (notches will save you).

3. Separate each muslin pattern piece, iron it flat, and re-mark lines if necessary.

4. Place each pattern piece face up on its own segment of pattern paper, securing it with small weights to prevent sliding.

5. Use a tracing wheel and carbon paper to transfer all the necessary markings from each muslin pattern piece onto pattern paper.

6. Lightly mark in seam lines with pencil, ruler, and curve tools.

7. Overlap pattern pieces to ensure that notches and seam lines align. Make any necessary corrections.

8. Label each pattern piece with the appropriate information: garment name, pattern piece, grain line, number of pieces to be cut ("cut 2 on fold"), and number of a pattern piece out of the entire group ("piece 7 of 15").

9. Lay the paper pattern on the final fabric. Weight, cut, pin, and sew.

DESIGN DETAILS
There are many elements that distinguish designer garments from the ones available at the local mall, although some features can be subtler than others. **Elaborate buttons and trim, luxe fabrics, and well-thought-out finishing are all elements that can be relatively recognizable features, but specialized components such as bound button holes, rolling lapels, complicated inner construction, and luxurious linings may warrant a closer look. When a designer creates a collection, it's important for every facet, no matter how large or minute, to be considered; from buttons to styling, linings to silhouette, all of the details must be covered.**

On *Project Runway*, adding subtle details and unique elements was a tricky part of the challenges, as there was no guarantee that the judges would even see them. I can recall numerous times when one of us would simply shout "I can't do it!" in the midst of the chaos because there just wasn't enough time for the small things. Self-editing was a painfully obvious part of the design process during the show (last-minute sewing, frantic camera movements, and a sweaty brow are usually safe indicators that this was going on), and if a designer overcommitted him- or herself to a design feature that simply couldn't be completed in time . . . it showed. Nevertheless, I do remember one of my favorite challenges, partway through season two: I took inspiration from an orchid and translated it into a diaphanous, floating blouse constructed from champagne-hued silk organza. I defined the waist by sewing column after column of 2-inch-high pin tucks, bringing in the loose organic shape but in an unexpected, high-end technique. I could have easily sewn in elastic to give the design an identical shape and silhouette, which surely would have saved me hours of work, but it would not have given the garment the finesse and polish I was aiming for.

When designing my latest collection, I knew that I wanted the design details to be clean and very modern. I am not traditionally drawn to excessive trim or loud prints, so I was hoping to bring in visual interest and contrast with textural variations. A subtle feature of Anna's party dress is the slightly oversized metallic outer collar. By creating the inside ever so slightly smaller than the outside, it gives the hard lines of the metallic collar a softer feel, making it feel a bit more organic and not so tech-y

This tiered ombré chiffon top was inspired by a rock wall comprised of layered slabs of slate that I had come across a few weeks earlier. It had rained the previous night and part of the rock was still wet, giving it a subtle, gradational hue. I wanted to translate the subtle changes in color and texture into the top, creating "soft texture" but also bringing lightness to the garment. Seen from afar, the top looks solid and single-layered, but on the body, in motion, it takes on the fluidity of water.

and harsh. I particularly like it when paired with the cleanliness of the green cotton sateen of the body; juxtaposing the two elements of hard and soft creates a small, unexpected friction in the look . . . and I love it! You may also notice the clear plastic straps on the evening gown and how they have a small strip of ombré silk chiffon sewn onto the underside, giving a varying texture but also a stunning gradation effect. I wanted the fade of the ombré to continue around the body, following the continuous fade of the rest of the dress, so when cutting the fabric I took extra care to place each strap on the ombré chiffon according to where it would be placed on the body . . . allowing for continuity throughout the design. All in all, design details are an interesting and important part of a designer's work; they should never solely dictate the design, but rather they should enhance it.

The inner construction of a garment is, to me, sometimes more interesting than the exterior. I enjoy flipping a coat or dress inside out to see what work went into it; it's oftentimes a great way to see how thorough a designer is in his or her work. A jacket lined in simple, inexpensive polyester certainly does the job, but nothing feels quite as nice and luxurious as silk charmeuse against your skin, or opting for the 100 percent cashmere coating over a poly/wool blend, or using crisscross stitches to better secure buttons over the more common parallel method; it's not just the high-end look and fashion-forward aesthetic that make

designer clothing special, but the subtle nuances that bump them into a category all their own. However, that said, a design can quickly become overwhelmed with gimmicky "design details" and overly fussy excess that end up looking heavy-handed or arbitrary. Granted, I do feel this conundrum ventures into personal taste territory; I do not agree that simply adding a few yards of expensive trim to a basic T-shirt is what designer clothing should be about.

Bound buttonholes, which have their raw edges encased by pieces of fabric or trim instead of stitches, are a design detail that I've personally come to recognize and appreciate in tailored garments; I feel that they quietly proclaim "tailoring expertise." However, you'll usually find a more common machine-worked buttonhole in most ready-to-wear coats and jackets, which is a perfectly suitable solution, though nothing special. A bound buttonhole takes extra time and effort and truly shows a depth of skill, giving the finished garment a subtle polish and refinement. Not every design element needs to slap you across the face to make an impact. Specialized buttons and unique closures are also excellent items that a designer can employ to keep things interesting, especially when noticed at close hand, such as when a customer is shopping and actually trying on the clothes. Subtlety has its place, and a jacket can feel extra special and memorable when the closure is a particularly stunning one that the customer sees only up close.

At this stage, it's great to finally see my designs on an actual body—particularly how they fit and move, and which design features work the best versus those that don't work at all. Sometimes a design detail must be changed when assessing the garment in its entirety: beading moved, a strap enlarged, or a closure substituted, for example.

WHAT'S SEW IMPORTANT?

When a designer is aiming to sell his or her work, even if it's on a fairly small scale, it's important for the clothing to have a polished, finished look. Although many designers are good sewers and try to save money by producing a small collection themselves, unfortunately that choice often results in that oh-so-obvious "handmade" look, even when it's unintended. In my opinion, working with a trained seamstress is really the only way to go: Her familiarity with a range of fabrics and comfort using professional-grade sewing and pressing machines mean that even the most basic designs will be well-constructed, which can only increase their sales potential (and possibly their price point).

A designer can network around to see if there are any seamstresses available and to assess the details of the job at hand, including quantities and timing. In general, designers are better off hiring someone to sew their garments, even if all they can afford is part-time help from a neighborhood housewife with experience sewing her and her children's clothing. Regardless of who's sewing, it's beneficial for both parties to walk through a new pattern step-by-step to ensure consistency.

I would also advise designers to work with a professional patternmaker. It is the main component of a design and the single biggest reason people choose *not* to buy something. There are numerous stories of young designers looking to save money by producing patterns themselves, but they are extremely time-consuming, and even the smallest adjustment can change a design, so most of these designers went back to a professional and chose to save a few dollars elsewhere. It takes time to find a patternmaker whom you truly love (and you should *love* him or her, as a good pattern can make or break a design), but the best come through referrals or networking. It takes years to learn some of the finer points of the process, and a truly great pattern will almost certainly be seen in the final garment.

If a designer is absolutely desperate to save money and cannot hire a professional seamstress or factory to produce his or her sample designs, then this may be a place to cut corners by doing it him- or herself. However, it's wise to be aware that these samples will dictate the *entire* process from this stage on, and if the cutting, sewing, or altering is off then it will continue to be off from that point. Also, these samples will be shown to buyers, editors, and the public, and a designer needs them to be absolutely pristine; an unprofessional collection is a total deal breaker.

It can take years of practical experience—or the invaluable hand-me-down knowledge from a wise grandmother—to really get to know the tricks of the trade. Because my grandmother was unavailable for this book, I have instead enlisted the help and expertise of patternmaking genius Ardeana Kirckof to share useful tips and tricks that she's collected throughout her career. You'll find them on page 102, after our interview. Some are for sewing, others for presentation, and hopefully *all* will be useful! **DV**

When I was first learning to sew, I was so intimidated by the power and speed of an industrial sewing machine, especially when compared to my home version. Now there's nothing quite like watching a professional seamstress fly through a garment in a fraction of the time that it used to take me!

ARDEANA KIRCKOF

THE INCOMPARABLE ARDEANA KIRCKOF IS AS ENERGETIC TOWARD DESIGN AS SHE IS EDUCATED, bringing an inimitable eye and years of hands-on experience to the patternmaking table. Ardeana grew up in Northern California and opened her small business in 1999, offering custom-designed couture clothing. She moved to New York in 2006 and began freelancing in the industry for Rocawear, Raven Tailored, and Nicolas Caito Studio as a couture draper and patternmaker. She currently works at Diane von Furstenberg (DVF) as head of production pattern design.

DV: Let's start with your background: How did you get to New York? I know you studied in France for a while.

AK: I have my undergraduate degree from UCLA in art, with an emphasis in textiles. I've always been interested in textiles. My mom's a quilter, so I have a background in sewing and patterns. My interest in textiles was in between art and design, but with too much design for art and also too artistic for design. So I started my own little business. I started sewing for people, some wedding dresses and special occasion dresses. I also got a two-year fashion degree in dressmaking and patternmaking out in Northern California. And then there was no industry in California so I said, I gotta move! So I came to New York and I freelanced for a while, and that's how I got to know the industry and meet people and find the right company. I met Nicolas Caito, and my experience with him was very good because I got the finesse education that I needed to be confident and a very strong draper. He studied at the École Syndicale de la Haute Couture—he's very rigorous with patterns and couture patterns and all the techniques associated with this. I was doing dressmaking before and I'd learned drafting and pattern drafting and I knew the techniques and formulas. I had a very good education. I did go to France and I did study textiles there, and fashion just kind of came together for me. And the couture element with patternmaking, the technical and the design coming together, was really how all of my interests were put into one.

DV: When you first started, what was your intention? What did you look for—was it just a job in the industry that could pay the bills?

AK: I was really open to anything. I wasn't so concerned about what or where, but I certainly did not want to work at a huge corporation, sitting at a desk. I really wanted variety: every day there's a new problem, every day there's something exciting to do, every day you figure out x and y equal z and what's the problem. I really like to troubleshoot and figure out problem solving, which is a large part of what I do, actually. Even when I drape, I take this two-dimensional idea and turn it into a three-dimensional dress. That's a lot of problem solving and I really, really enjoy that. So that's how I ended up here. And I just ended up at DVF—they hired me on.

DV: You've said that, more important than a job title, you were instead chasing the atmosphere and more or less what you *wanted* in a job, not a specific job. That's great, because I think a lot of younger people have a clear idea of the job title they want, but they don't really understand what that person actually does.

AK: That's correct. There are so many facets of fashion, and so I knew that it was a very complicated process. I knew there were a lot of departments—there's sales, there's PR, there's marketing, there's the whole Web phenomenon, there's production, there's design. And I personally tend to like being behind the stage. I like building sets. I don't need to be onstage. I didn't need the spotlight. I'm actually not a spotlight-oriented person. I find it rewarding when I see my work coming down the runway without it actually being my dress, or my idea; I see the work I put into it. I don't need the name; that isn't important to me. I think a lot of people now kind of want—

DV: Just to be famous and not do the work.

AK: Yes. In design there's a lot of competition; you don't get a lot of money, and in other areas there's less competition and you can make money.

DV: Absolutely. That's a very good thing for young people to know going into this industry.

AK: In fashion there are a lot of designers, so to be a designer you have to be extremely talented, you have to be connected. It's really hard to come out of school and just get a job. You might have to intern, work your way up, make connections, show you are good designer, be able to function as the company wants you to.

DV: Can you tell us more specifically what you do in your position right now?

AK: Mostly problem solving and troubleshooting. Production and technical design is about second-guessing. We have to keep the vision of the designers. We also have to make this pattern in these clothes viable for the mass market and consumer. On the runway they're exaggerated for effect—they're beautiful, they've got the style, the models, but maybe not a lining!

DV: Which is why I always have to assure people at home that it's going to be altered for the sales floor—she won't have a completely sheer dress with no bra.

AK: Exactly. So we have to figure out, how do we put a lining inside this garment? Do we put a slip under it? We don't want the slip to show, so how do we do that? There are too many pleats in the shoulders, we need to decrease that. Do we move it? Do we take them away? These are all questions that come up, so it's actually quite complicated. I think this is the definition of good design—it looks effortless.

There's a lot of work that goes into it, and people don't realize how much work there is. There are two or three fit samples. There's a lot of decision making in terms of the designer's vision and design integrity. The designers are usually at the initial fitting: "Okay, these pleats can be removed," or "Let's take away 20 percent of the sweep." In production they look at the garment and say, "We have to line this dress or there's no way we can have a skirt this full," or "It's too costly to produce; how do we find a less expensive way to produce this?" or "How will we produce this handmade item for the mass market?" So these are all decisions that have to be made. And that's what's interesting, is taking this idea and really paring it down and streamlining it, and nobody knows how much work actually does go into that.

DV: And it's not just making it viable for the customer; it's keeping the integrity of the design.

AK: And it's a very slippery slope, because sales has certain requirements: "We want pockets, we want pockets, we want pockets"—and if they get complaints about the dresses being too hippy—"No pockets, no pockets, no pockets." So sales has input, design has input, and production has input. It's a wheel with all these spokes on it, and if there's no spoke in that wheel, it's not going to ride down the road.

DV: Tell me about the pattern work you're doing now.

AK: I'm fixing the development patterns for production: What is the problem with this? Why is the side seam not working? Why are our buttonholes funny every time? How come the side seams are swinging forward? Because I have the training now and the eye to spot it. I can figure it out. I know how to balance patterns. I know how to do all this stuff. I deal with factories; I explain to them the problem and how to fix it. I have a lot of technical experience and also just experience in dealing with this job and problem solving in general.

DV: So you can say that you're *still* learning while you're on the job, right?

AK: Of course. You never stop learning. There's always something new. There's always something challenging. There's always some way to do something different. There are really no rules.

DV: What draws you to certain designers?

AK: Innovative design, progressive thinking. I tend to like people who are visionary—DVF because she does support her designers, and all of her textile designs are original. Her designers are very original, so that was very important to me. I've worked at a number of companies where they just ripped off clothes. It's a very common practice in the industry. I don't care for that. It's not interesting to me. I need to be inspired. I also just like the working environment, and interacting with my coworkers is very important. That is what feels inspirational. And when I was doing the wedding and the social occasion dresses, my customers came to me with their ideas and we worked on them together.

DV: Oh, a bride is a challenging customer!

AK: Well, it was such a collaboration—collaboration is very important to me in terms of my vision, meaning that I think a collaboration makes the strongest product. I like the creative process as a collaboration. I like to work very much as part of a group.

DV: On a somewhat different note, in your work and in your daily life, what inspires you? You're here in New York, you work in a very glamorous industry where you see some pretty fabulous things every day, but where else do you go to be inspired?

AK: I see it everywhere. And I'm not being stupid or trite about it, but it's a point of view. It's an openness to being inspired by anything and everything—to be open to different things and look differently. Just to look at the architecture, to see the ironwork, to take a picture, to pull out your cell phone and use your camera and to look at the trees when they're changing—all this stuff is really amazing—to go to the museum, to get out there.

DV: That's one of the things I'm trying to instill in my readers, is that you have to train your eye for it to come from anywhere.

AK: Oh, yes.

DV: Can you remember one thing that still speaks to you years later? Is there something specific?

AK: Well, being kind of a technical person, when I see people's clothes or see mine, I think, "Wow, that was a fantastic idea." I also think learning by imitation is a great way to learn. You know, in art class—or you see in the Metropolitan Museum these students copying. I think it's a great way to learn because when you imitate, you bring your own perspective and you improve it. There is this metaphor of architecture and building as it relates to fashion.

DV: Between fashion and art?

AK: Well, between construction and design. When a designer gives me a design, you're looking for some architectural information, you are an architect with a drawing: How do you build it? What kind of structure is going to make this happen? My point is that I can be just a builder, I have these skills, but I also happen to know how the structure works, how I can take your vision and improve by good structure, good bones, or a good foundation. I liked working with you because you are very open to hearing how you can improve your design by quality materials, a good base, or the proper pattern work. Some people simply want a builder: "These are my technical specifications, and just do it." So I think that to be inspired you need to have this ability to grow, to collaborate and imitate, reference, and be open.

DV: So looking at what has happened before your step in the process, and what's going to follow your step, is important because if it was just the builder there may be no forward thinking in it.

AK: Exactly. And there're certain people who are very good builders, but I think if you want to be inspired you have to step forward or take the step backward and just goof around. I think that's a good life philosophy, to always seek and find inspiration. I think you either have design inspiration or you don't and you choose to develop it. That's what made me think of architecture. Either you're an architect or you're a builder and you can be an architect but you have to develop it. You have to train yourself.

DV: Is there anything that you could say now with your experience?

AK: I think I'd have to say, do everything. The whole process is so important and what you learn along the way. I wish designers were better patternmakers and better at understanding the whole philosophy of clothes and construction and not necessarily just the glamorous vision of clothes. Just the rules you pick up along the way are really important, like cracking the bias, like hanging that bias the night before to get it to drip before you lay the pattern out so it's already done, it's cracked.

DV: I'm grateful to know you, Ardeana. Thank you.

Sewing

When inserting a vertical zipper on bias fabric, iron in fusible interfacing (it also comes in clear) just on the seam line and inside, so the zipper won't become stiff and wavy.

Bias stretches ¼" per 6"; a pattern should not be altered to adjust to this, but the bias needs to hang before cutting. The night before, attach the material on the bias to a door, using a safety pin and hanger, and let the bias crack (a term Vionnet used to describe the change in fabric). Then you can lay out the pattern. There shouldn't be wavy seams if it is done correctly.

Use the slightest zigzag stitch when sewing velvet, as it minimizes puckering.

To ease excess by machine, pin the dress tape at the beginning and end of the seam. Pin continuously in between, halving the pin distance each time until the dress tape is secured; there will be slight bubbles in between. When sewing, keep the tape on top; the pressure of the sewing machine will stretch the top layer and pull the bottom layer through.

Always use dress tape along the neckline—whether it be a sweetheart neck, V-neck, or rounded neck—to stay the neck seam and keep it from stretching. Cut the tape ¼" less than the measured neckline and ease it in.

On strapless or strappy dresses, you can make the stay tape that runs above the bust (keeping the dress from stretching) ³⁄₈" less than center front to side seam. This will ease in the bodice, as well as cup the bustier over the bust curve so it doesn't flop open.

Tips from
Ardeana Kirckof
PATTERNMAKER

Always test designs in muslin first, stitching the garment using a long stitch length (for ease when/if taking it apart later) and 1" seam allowances (its easier to take away than it is to add!), and always use good cotton thread: it's more durable than polyester versions.

Inner Construction
Organza underlining strengthens the

garment, giving structure while keeping it light. It can be used on everything from wedding dresses to wool coats. It goes in between the lining and the fashion fabric.

A great way to ease a sleeve cap is to use a bias strip of wool. You can use fluffy mohair wool or wool felt; double it up to keep the sleeve cap from puckering and collapsing. Baste it in first by hand, stretching it to ease in the sleeve cap and give support.

For a nice cowl drape you can use a fabric-covered weight (or a fabric-covered dime or penny) and tuck it inside the cowl facing. Stitch it on with a chain stitch, the way a coat lining is attached to the inside seam. This will keep the drape hanging nicely. (Elie Tahari does this.)

Shoulder pads can be made from a needle punch,

which can be found in a quilting store. It is about $1/8$" thick and you can use one to three layers, depending on the structure, to achieve the desired thickness and shape.

Presentation

Make sure to clip your seams within $1/16$ of the stitching line to avoid puckering when finished. Where the garment will be clipped (on the neck curve, bust seam, armhole, etc.), use a shorter stitch length, as this will strengthen the seam. Clip the threads after the stitch is finished (sloppy hanging threads can destroy a garment).

For strappy straps, cut the strips on bias and turn them right side out. If you don't have a fast-turn tool, attach a small safety pin to one end and work it through the tube,

giving you something heftier to grab on to. Place the straps on the ironing board with a pin at both ends, stretching them as taut as you can. Steam press and let them sit. You can do this more than once to steam out all of the bias and get really good spaghetti straps.

Grain line is so important. When placing your

pattern on fabric, use the selvage edge of the fabric as a guideline, placing a clear plastic ruler on the marked grain line on the pattern and making sure it is the exact distance at the top and bottom from the selvage edge. If designs are unintentionally sewn off-grain, the final garment will twist and warp.

Steam pressing as you sew is crucial. Use a

light press at first and then give the final garment a good pressing at the end. Many mediocre sewing projects can be saved with exquisite pressing. A good steam iron is preferable; an investment in an industrial-grade iron will change your world.

When pressing wool, steam press it, use a wooden press board, and let the wool dry a minute or two before moving it. This will solidify the seam and make it really crisp.

Gabardine is the most unforgiving fabric but it

presses beautifully. However, you can press it only one time, as the press mark will always be there.

To set a seam, use a mixture of 2 tablespoons white wine vinegar to 1 cup of water. Put it into a spray bottle, spray the seam, and press. You can also remove seams using this mixture (if a dress needs to be let out and you don't want the stitching lines to show, this works especially well with natural fibers like wool and silk).

I've heard that you can remove a used-garment smell by spritzing cheap vodka on the garment. The vodka absorbs the odor and leaves no residue.

THE
WHOLE LOOK

STYLING FASHION

NO ONE CAN DENY THAT IMAGE IS A HUGE PART OF THE FASHION INDUSTRY. IT'S IMPORTANT THAT EVERY STAGE OF THE FASHION PROCESS, EVEN THOSE BEYOND PURE INSPIRATION AND DESIGN—from runway shows to magazine covers and ads, from a celebrity on the red carpet to retail merchandising—represent the designer's point of view. Designers are by definition creative beings (or should be), with the ability to assess and define their own work at each step in its development, but sometimes it's necessary to call for backup, and often it's a fashion stylist who gets the first call.

At times, designers look to far-off lands and obscure references for inspiration for their collections, and regardless of whether the customer sees the initial inspiration, it really comes down to whether they like the clothing, and understand it. Stylists can help designers focus and edit their ideas, not only giving individual looks a personal touch but the collection as a whole a precise and forward-thinking edge. Even at the beginning stages of a budding design career, it's important for a designer to have a cohesive look and distinct point of view, and whether that's styling the looks for a runway show, shooting a look book or advertising campaign, or suggesting the strongest pieces to offer celebrities to wear, stylists can help. At times, a designer is more focused on the micro elements of a collection—the cut, the fit, the detailing—while a stylist can bring a fresh perspective, objectively reviewing the overall style in order to fit it into the broader fashion spectrum. The relationship of a designer and a stylist can be measured in varying degrees; some designers do all their own styling, while others feel the need to have the assistance of someone who has his or her finger on fashion's pulse. Stylists can offer guidance and a new perspective to designers on what's currently happening on the street or in pop culture, helping to keep the collections looking modern and fresh. Having that second set of trained eyes that have the means and know-how to assess the ever-changing winds of style can be extremely helpful in the fast-paced world of fashion, as some designers are focused so intently on the collection as a whole.

To me, the phrase "to style" means to define a look. Stylists must take elements from the past, present, and future and constantly create new and exciting ways of seeing them. With increasing regularity, stylists work closely with designers at various stages of the process to help ensure cohesiveness and a "plotline" in a collection. Some stylists go so far as to land design positions at fashion companies, overseeing entire collections as creative directors, while others branch out into the editorial world, contributing ideas for shoot locations, stories, and clothing choices for glossy fashion spreads. Such style manipulators as former *Vogue* and *Allure* editor Polly Mellon, French *Vogue* editor-in-chief Carine Roitfeld, *Vogue* creative director Grace Coddington, and *W* magazine's senior contributing fashion editor Camilla Nickerson have all worked with some of the best and well-known designers and photographers from around the globe, creating stunning images and memorable moments. They have all gone on to become key players in the fashion industry, employing their endless creativity and undying passion for fashion.

still contributing to outside projects as well. Their job is to show what's new in fashion at that moment, in exciting and unique ways, while a celebrity stylist is probably more concerned with landing his or her client on "best dressed" lists over pushing the limits of the avant-garde. When it comes to designers honing their vision for a runway show or ad campaign, it really is up to the designers to choose a stylist who they think best follows their understanding. That said, I repeat that not every designer wants or *needs* a stylist. One drawback is that, if a stylist is working for multiple clients, the final products tend to look quite similar and more like the stylist's vision than the designer's.

During my stint on *Project Runway*, there wasn't much time left after designing and sewing to consider styling options before we hurriedly sent our looks down the runway, but thanks to sponsors we were provided with shoes, bags, and belts to choose from. It was crucial to complete the look with whatever we had available, and that included making your own accessories if you had the time, creating a unique hairstyle or makeup story, and, of course, developing an appropriately fierce walk for the runway (some models can sell *anything*). Granted, adding accessories just for the sake of adding sometimes backfired; it's hard to get anything with a questionable taste level past the judges' keen eyes!

Stylists like James DeMolet, whom you'll meet on page 112, often spend countless hours packing trunks with clothing, cataloging garments, and lugging suitcases filled with accessories to the farthest-reaching locations . . . definitely working hard to live the "glamorous" life.

editorial stylists "call in" pieces that they'd like to use for photo shoots—everything from $20,000 gowns to $2 charms—which are then cataloged, shot, and returned quickly (maybe with a few pestering phone calls to help things along) and undamaged (one hopes). The arrangement is essentially a loan: In exchange for the temporary use of the item, the designer receives exposure in the publication, usually in the form of a clothing credit. Designers typically produce anywhere from one to three samples of each piece each season (depending on how large the company and the extent of its press capabilities) for the purpose of loaning them out for promotional opportunities. There's a hierarchy in the fashion industry that, at times, can be difficult to navigate. Of course it's easier for larger design houses, which have more staff and resources than smaller ones, to participate in this arrangement, and naturally it's easier for magazines with well-known names and bigger audiences to borrow pieces from Gucci, for example, than it is for a free alternative weekly.

For red carpet or other events with major press attendance, such as the Academy Awards or the Grammys, the roles are reversed, with designers competing to have well-known celebrities (or the hottest new starlets) wear their gowns. Stylists suddenly become an eager designer's best friend in hopes that the stylist will push his or her gowns as an option to A-list clients. For celebrities, it can be as easy as trying on one dress, regardless of who sent it; if it looks good and they feel great, then everyone wins. In recent years, such big-name designers as Giorgio Armani have even set up camp in Los Angeles the week prior to the Academy Awards to help prep and pamper the celebrities who have agreed to answer the red-carpet question "Who are you wearing?" with their brand. Predictably, every year rumors of design houses "bribing" celebrities to choose their latest couture confections emerge, though thankfully not all stylists and designers play that way. In most cases, the designer/stylist/client connection is a win-win situation, especially when a relationship develops between the right duo at the right time: Sofia Coppola and Marc Jacobs, Charlotte Gainsbourg and Nicolas Ghesquière, Rachel Weisz and Narciso Rodriguez. Obviously, this relationship is especially advantageous to the designers, who get free publicity, but it's not without its pitfalls. In a time when even the launch of a new video game system becomes a red-carpet event, having your label represented by the "wrong" person can be a tricky situation. A few years ago, a few days after Karl Lagerfeld held his couture show for Chanel, rocker Courtney Love was seen attending a party wearing one of the looks that was shown on the runway just days earlier. Chanel was thoroughly confused as to how one of their newest samples made it across the ocean from their showroom and onto Courtney Love's back,

SECRETS OF SUCCESSFUL STYLING

When searching for resources for styling my designs, my mantra is "use your mind before your wallet," not solely for economic reasons but for the boundaries it creates for me. **I'm aiming to solve the problem at hand with some ingenuity and, I hope, to present my designs from a fresh perspective.**

It can take years of diligent work before designers and showrooms finally open their doors to a stylist, as not everyone wants to lend their clothing to just anyone. With thorough experience, the right attitude, and a great eye, a stylist will soon see his or her options multiply.

In styling, it's those untraditional pairings that can create new and exciting looks or intriguing silhouettes: Suddenly the belt becomes a bracelet, a sweater gets tied into a scarf, an antique pin becomes a hair clip—and it all begins to evolve into something fresh and novel. Though we'd all love to have a huge, Mariah Carey–sized closet full of the world's most glamorous shoes to choose from, using whatever resources are right in front of you sometimes yields more interesting results. I've seen a pair of worn, ratty shoes bought for $5 at the Salvation Army spray-painted, shellacked, polished, and buffed into the most stunning pair of beauties imaginable; a fellow designer used them when shooting a look book for her latest collection, filled with vintage, boudoir-inspired designs that were complemented perfectly by the shoes. I watched a stylist friend take apart handfuls of earrings with no mates and string them together with strips of chiffon to create absolutely gorgeous necklaces an hour before a photo shoot because the alternative jewelry wasn't working. Raiding a friend's/parent's/lover's closet can become quite the rewarding treasure hunt (just either ask first or be very, *very* quiet when they're in the other room). One of my friends wears a shrunken navy schoolboy blazer she found at a local thrift shop and embellished with some new buttons and contrasting trim, and it's become one of the most talked-about pieces in her wardrobe.

By styling their finds—wherever they're found—in new and unexpected ways, designers can create memorable images that will inspire not just themselves but those around them, enabling them to stand out from the rest. The process is similar to gathering inspiration. Spending time at the movies or an afternoon people-watching in the park, or looking at every visual reference possible, from *National Geographic* to an illustrated edition of *Grimm's Fairy Tales*, are great ways to stretch creativity. By training themselves to notice things that provoke a reaction, regardless of the source, designers help fuel those bursts of creative energy that their work requires: The shocking colors of an Amazonian flower in full bloom may translate beautifully into a makeup story, or the regal styling of a French renaissance painting could be a jumping-off point when styling a runway show—as long as the story always supports the design.

Some of the world's most successful designers style their looks in extreme ways to get a season's particular message across. I recall reading an interview with the infamously talented makeup artist Pat McGrath in which she described a conversation she had had with John Galliano before one of his colossal shows for Dior. The collection being shown was full of retro 1940s references: a strong shoulder, nipped-in waist, and slim pencil skirts, all of which were infused with Galliano's signature in-your-face flair. Their resulting makeup concept was about an early '40s woman who got locked in her closet with only her makeup case and a pocket mirror, and day after day she would apply and reapply her makeup, until sixty years later, when the runway show was actually taking place. Although the image it created—bold red lips, bleached-out face, and extremely heavy brows—could never be worn on the street, it's an example of how styling clothes with bold makeup can be an effective way of getting their message across and help make them, and the collection, memorable.

When styling the collection featured in this book, I wanted the choices to be clean, modern, and sleek, so I kept an eye out for pieces that would work with my original inspiration. Clear plastic jewelry, metallic headbands and bracelets, and chunky, patent-leather footwear were all thrown into the suggestion bin, but as I tried different pieces with each of the looks, I began to feel that less was more. I knew what I wanted the final photographs of the collection to look like—extreme wind, metallic leaves, and stumbling posture, all to show movement—and the more I thought about

it, the more I felt that some of my initial choices would make the images too busy: A simple shoe would seem too delicate, a pair of earrings would distract from the model's skin and hair. I finally decided that going with a bold, graphic shoe—and nothing else—would help fix the model in the midst of the planned chaos, while injecting some visual contrast among the gradated colors and tones of the garments and background. I ran styling options past a few fashion friends of mine, but in the end I really wanted to tackle this one on my own. I knew how I wanted the final images to look and felt that since I already knew which pieces I wanted to shoot, I had a good understanding as to how the whole image would read. In the end, a designer should always trust his or her instincts—no one knows your vision better than you.

JAMES DEMOLET

JAMES WORTHINGTON DEMOLET IS A NEW YORK CITY—BASED STYLIST who studied at the Fashion Institute of Technology and London's Central St. Martins College of Art & Design. He was on staff at *Teen Vogue* until the fall of 2007, when he left to style for other publications. While he continues to style for *Teen Vogue*, he has since contributed to a range of publications, including *i-D*, *Celeste*, *GQ*, *Interview*, and *NYLON*. As an assistant he has worked with an illustrious list of fashion editors. James has never been afraid to get down and dirty to get the job done. He shared with me how his determined attitude, creative intuition, and growing résumé have helped him work his way up in the fashion industry, as well as some advice for aspiring fashion stylists.

DV: What role does a stylist play when working editorially as well as with a designer?

JD: The largest codependent relationship that exists in the fashion industry is that between the stylist and the designer. Many designers aren't able to make decisions without the input of their stylist. There is an increasing number of editorial stylists who have taken the title of "creative director" at major design houses because their part in the line is so much more than that of a stylist. The stylist is the one who is brought in to interpret the pieces as something relevant to current and future trends. The stylist is also expected to understand the targeted customer and arrange the clothing in a way that this customer can best understand. In working with designers, young designers especially, it can be exciting to help them to create the image of the brand. This image should be concise and developed before the public is made aware of the brand. These concepts should be developed even before fashion insiders hear of the brand. The most successful brands and designers are those who have a clear concept of who and what they are. Brands that continue to be newsworthy and directional—in a good way—are those that grasp where fashion is going, and it is often the stylist who helps the designer understand this concept.

DV: How important is it to match the right model/styling/mood to the right designer?

JD: Young designers should always remember that models become the faces of their collection, and when they're casting they should keep this in mind. Recall certain brands, and for most of them you will think of who the face of their campaign was, or who opened their show. Oftentimes this face is easier to mentally recall than the face of the designer. I enjoy knowing who the designer is, but in photos I would prefer to see who they choose to wear their designs. When I cast models I aim to work with boys and girls who are fascinating, current, and somewhat timeless. To use a girl who is too trendy or too editorially of the moment can date the photos.

DV: What models have inspired you in the past?

JD: Coco Rocha. The word *fierce* is beyond overused, but when you see her walk in a show you understand where it came from. She has such an intriguing strength in her face that I find quite inspiring. Her breadth of work continues to amaze me; she understands theatrics better than any model her age. During Fashion Week recently I was sitting on one of the park benches in Bryant Park and I saw a young girl (clearly a model) in gray drainpipes, a light coat, and red studded Louboutins (about half a size too large) running to the subway. It wasn't until someone stopped her to snap a photo that I realized it was Coco. Although she was clearly running late for another show, she gladly stopped for a photo and brief chat. You forget when looking at her photos that she is still just a young girl. She seems quite grounded, and I will always find that more inspiring than cheekbones! Coco has had a long history in the performing arts that has given her a great understanding of theatrics. I love working with girls who have an understanding of theatrics but know how to adjust it to their client, whether it be a publication or designer.

DV: How does a young designer go about making connections and trying to network?

JD: Interning. It's the most honest form of networking. When you hear "networking" you think of something a bit more social, but I think young creatives trying to make connections in fashion should *always* start interning. Also, go to school in New York—you'll find that when you graduate you continue to work with the people in your class . . . so be nice! No matter how they were in school, if they get a job in the industry, chances are you'll run into them.

DV: Do you have any suggestions for young designers trying to get their work seen/shot about where to go and whom to talk to?

JD: Again, intern. I can't stress this enough—intern as much as possible! Alexander Wang is a great example of how being a great intern can affect the growth of your line as a young designer. He is a Parsons design graduate who interned at *Teen Vogue* and *Vogue* magazines, and from what I heard he was a great help and had a strong personality; thus, he was memorable. When he launched his impeccable line of knitwear his first customers were editors. I'm sure those editors to whom Wang gifted these knits were probably the first to shoot them. While there are many other ways of getting to know editors and informing them of your work, this way can be the most redeeming. If you work your ass off helping them pack trunks, prepare for shoots, return clothing, and all the other annoying things that interns have to handle, when you decide to launch your line the editors owe it to you to check it out. They all know this, and I can't think of one editor whom I've worked with who wouldn't agree with me. If any of my former interns (who really worked hard, mind you!) launched a line of clothing, I would absolutely owe it to them to check it out, and I'd do my very best to shoot it.

NICO ACEVES

NICO ACEVES IS A SOUTHERN CALIFORNIA NATIVE WHO MOVED TO NEW YORK CITY IN EARLY 2000. He has established himself as a top hairstylist at Bumble and bumble and as a lead educator at the salon's Bb University. Nico is also a key presence backstage during New York Fashion Week. Sharing memorable stories from past fashion moments is always a good time, especially when they're with someone who has seen it all. Nico gave me some behind-the-scenes scoop along with his view on the role of a hairstylist as part of the greater fashion machine.

DV: What does your job entail on a daily basis?

NA: On a daily basis my job entails cutting hair. I'm also an educator, so I teach part of the time. So half my time is spent in the salon and the other half is spent educating stylists from around the country that are in our network.

DV: What about during Fashion Week—what are your duties then?

NA: For the whole week I'm pretty much backstage doing hair and assisting the art editorial team. We're pretty much on call the whole week. We do get a schedule ahead of time, and luckily our team is getting bigger, so the schedule's getting easier for us. But for the most part the salon represents close to forty shows. I was only at about a quarter of those shows, one or two shows at most per day. So it wasn't overwhelming. The way that works is, we have a group of editorial stylists who generally work in the salon part-time and then do photo shoots or on-set work the rest of the time. They're the ones who get the gigs, who have the relationships with the designers, or the connections where their work is being seen more in magazines, so those designers seek them out. They collaborate weeks before, days before, however long it takes. They decide on a look, we show up, and in essence we're like their assistants.

DV: Generally speaking, how important a role do hair, hairstylists, and haircuts play in a designer's vision?

NA: It's very, very, important—that role is definitely one to be taken seriously. In general, whether it's a shoot or a fashion show, there are so many different people operating to bring the look together, and each part of the collaborating process is equally important. But it's teamwork. It's definitely not just about you. And sometimes you have to take a step down and realize you need to work with these other individuals and take criticism from them as well. It is collaboration. A lot of times, a designer already knows exactly what they want. There's also a clothing stylist who tends to have more direction in terms of what is going to be the look or the theme of the shoot. But it just depends.

DV: **Where do you find inspiration?**

NA: I feel like inspiration can be found anywhere; you just have to keep your eyes open, but you also continuously have to think. You have to make sure that you visit other museums or exhibits, and you do have to look through all the current magazines just to see what is out there. It helps to also see other people's work. It just comes from so many places. Living in New York it's almost given to you so easily, and that's great, but it's also something that you have to see. In New York, with the number of people here, you sometimes are able to find it in someone else, whether it's something that they're wearing or a way that they style their hair for the day—people take it to the extreme, and you're able to see that on many faces. But otherwise you do have to go out and seek it. Obviously fashion is a very good place to start as well, but even fashion is borrowed from music. It's just such a cool circle.

DV: **We know that New York is filled with stimuli all the time. For readers who may not be in the big fashion capitals, what else can you suggest?**

NA: Exhibitions and magazines, but even then, it's so much about other references as well. You really have to be able to look, perhaps at books from the past to see if you can borrow a reference and make it your own. So that's definitely one place I think is a great place to start—not to copy, but to borrow, to reference, from the past.

DV: **Do you have any suggestions for young hairstylists and designers trying to get their work shot and shown— whether in New York or elsewhere?**

NA: The way that it worked for me—and it really can be done anywhere—is by seeking a hairstylist to collaborate with; it's as easy as going to a salon and asking. You can speak to someone who is in training, and that's how you develop the relationship and can grow together. So it's almost like finding someone at your level and seeing if they're willing to work with you, and then you just grow with them from there. Sometimes it's as easy as finding an assistant at another salon or someone who's already starting to shoot as a photographer and is in need of a test and is in need of experience. So whether it's someone who's starting out or has already been doing hair for a while and is interested in

doing editorial, you really have to be able to open your mind and see things in a different way, especially with those European magazines. They take it so extreme and sometimes you have to filter that stuff down, whether you share it with a client for day-to-day work or you transform it and make it your own. But one thing that I do want to say is it all comes down to technique, for sure. You definitely have to know your basics and to know how to be able to use product and how to manipulate hair. But from there it's a matter of practicing it. You have to continuously practice those basics, and then you start to expand and build on them and just take them in different directions.

DV: **Because a lot of people see a final product in magazines . . .**

NA: . . . and they copy it right away—you have to start from the ground up.

THE RIGHT
MODELS
Whether a designer is casting for her twenty-fifth runway show in Bryant Park or snapping a Polaroid of a dress he made in his living room, it's extremely important to choose the right model. I would love to say that people shouldn't be judged by what they look like, but until we live in a world where that's the reality, we have to acknowledge our society's ideal that tall and skinny equate to beautiful and inspirational. Call it what you want—a complex, a social norm, or maybe just brainwashing—it is what it is. I personally think the concept originated decades ago, when top-tier, designer-level clothing was thought to look its best displayed on only the rarest of beauties. Women who fit the standard model measurements make up less than 1 percent of the human population . . . what's rarer than that? As I mentioned in Chapter 1, when sketching elongated fashion figures, as well as showing designs on tall, slender models for a runway show, the image evokes an air of grace, beauty, and exoticism; I think the modern ideal of beauty, what we know today, has and will continue to evolve with social influence.

The modeling industry hasn't been the most culturally diverse business, although recently the range of skin tones has increased and the definition of "ideal beauty" on the runways has broadened. At any rate, it's a cyclical business and, from Brazilian bombshells to brooding Eastern European beauties, models will always reflect the fashions of the season. During the "supermodel" era of Cindy, Naomi, Linda, and Christy, where each was a one-name star in her own right, the models looked like women and exuded a strong, powerful demeanor—it was more about the girl than what she was wearing. Then followed a backlash, marking the Kate Moss/heroin chic era, where models weren't much more than walking boards and any woman who looked older than a prepubescent twelve-year-old boy seemed out of place. The tide turned yet again when doe-eyed, ethereal beauties like Daria Werbowy, Natalia Vodianova, and Gemma Ward began gracing every magazine cover and runway around the world, bringing an innocent, almost angelic look that the industry had never seen before.

When choosing models, designers should think first and foremost about which girl will represent *their brand and their vision*, rather than the flavor of the season—though if the two are the same, all the better! Whether it's the cute and perky blonde next door or the bold African beauty with the legs that go on for days, the choice should be bold and consistent with the designer's point of view. A photograph in a magazine that features a striking model will most certainly grab (and keep) the reader's attention more effectively than a conventional-looking one.

When I was looking at models to cast for the collection in this book, to help narrow my search I began by thinking of a few important characteristics that my ideal model needed:

* To be able to use her body well (possibly jumping, falling, and so on)
* To have a bold look (with a beautiful face *and* a great body)
* An engaging personality (a must!)

So I asked my good friend José Covarrubias (see our interview on page 118), an agent at Elite Model Management, to send over a package with my requirements (this can be an actual package, but it's mostly sent digitally nowadays), including the date we were shooting. José sent me information for twelve girls he thought would work for the project. At this point in the process, it becomes a matter of editing: seeing who grabs your attention immediately (and who keeps it), noting whom else she has shot with—

that is, which magazines and photographers, which are a good indication of her potential if she's new to the scene—and the range of her work. My first choice was Todiana, an amazingly awkward, 5-foot, $10\frac{1}{2}$-inch beauty with long brown hair (which I had requested), mile-long legs, and the most gorgeous long neck I've ever seen (perfect for all the high necklines in the collection!). I called to confirm with José that she was available, asked her rate, and told him that I would call back within the next few hours to make it official. Well, to show how fast things move in this industry, when I called back two hours later I was informed that my top choice had just been booked for a major hair campaign. Damn. If I had been able to throw down Gucci-sized money then this story would have had a different ending, but unfortunately I had to head back to the drawing board.

Lo and behold, José sent me a new model who had recently been moved up within the agency from the aptly named Fresh Faces division to the highly competitive, much higher stakes Women's board, a truly striking girl by the name of Lee Greene. I liked her portfolio but was stunned to see her that her hair was not only *short* but *bleached blonde* . . . still, I liked her look. So it was decision-making time again: Would my original concept still work, or would it have to evolve? Did I give Lee the boot and use someone else? Or did I throw on a pair of heels from the drag store down the block and model everything myself?! Thankfully, despite my initial hesitation, Lee was amazing. Not only was she gorgeous to look at but a dream to work with, improvising with movement and shape while still taking direction from both Michael and me. These sorts of things happen all the time, even with big-name clients, fighting it out for the same top girls each season, putting their agents in the difficult position of wanting to please many but ultimately having to leave someone with their second, or even third, choice.

JOSÉ COVARRUBIAS

JOSÉ COVARRUBIAS IS A MODEL SCOUT AND BOOKER FOR ELITE MODEL MANAGEMENT. **Having traveled the world as a performer, a chance meeting with the former director of Elite led José to a brief stint as a production assistant during the "New Faces" of Elite launch, where he was handpicked to join the development team at Elite.** José books not only the stars of tomorrow but also some of the stars of today, such as Jaslene Gonzalez and Caridee English, both winners of *America's Next Top Model*. In the short time that José has been with Elite, this San Diego native has traveled all over the globe, scouting for new talent in places such as Milan, Paris, and Russia. Managing the lives and careers of fashion models can become an all-consuming experience, but hearing the real story from José about what really happens behind the glitz and glamour helped to give me a bit more perspective.

DV: What is your role here at Elite Model Management, and what does that entail?

JC: My official title is "New Faces and Scouting." So what I do is help develop and find new talent around the world. And what I do as a "new face" booker is send the girls out to get pictures and meet new clients and get established in New York before—hopefully after a minimum of two years—moving them onto the other boards.

DV: Speaking of moving onto the other boards, what's a common cycle for most models?

JC: That's a good question. For baby models, say still in high school, we say that they're going to be a new face until they graduate, until they can be a full-time model, and then they can go onto the main board—the direct board. But when they're still in school, that's when we step in and it's part-time modeling; you have to tackle their class schedule, you have to handle their parents, you have to handle their spring breaks. And their summer break is when we have an influx of many, many girls from all over the world.

DV: How many divisions do you have at Elite?

JC: We have Scouting, New Faces, and Direct Board, which is actually like the money catalog board, where the women are all over the world but they're booked directly so they don't have to necessarily live in New York. So they already have the clientele. The Main Board is the girls who come from New Faces and they have a clientele base and they're doing editorial—traveling the world doing fashion weeks. And then we have "Elite plus" which I kind of call "plus models": *plus* actress, *plus* singer, *plus*—

DV: Ah, beauties who can talk, sing, and/or dance!

JC: That's like a less celebrity division. And then we have Showroom or Runway, which is our hidden moneymaker. It's fittings, showroom clients . . . all the stuff that everybody hates but makes a lot of money at.

DV: I think for most people outside our industry, they immediately equate a glossy magazine spread with fame and fortune. Could you elaborate on that?

JC: It's great to be on a billboard, it's great to be in a magazine, it's great to be in all these editorial magazines, but those are not going to pay your bills. The girls —they pay their rent, and they pay back their agency, and they pay back their debt by doing catalogs, by doing commercial work, by doing Internet stuff, by doing showroom, look books, things for trade.

DV: In your opinion, what role does a model play in a designer's vision? And that includes things such as editorial and runway. How important is a good rapport between the two—is it underestimated or overestimated? Is a girl just a girl?

JC: I think it's underestimated. It depends on the designer, too. The bigger the designer, that means it's whatever the "flavor of the week" is for that season. The smaller designers, by fitting the person for the first time and then starting a relationship with them, then they're probably going to use that person over and over again.

DV: I can certainly attest to that.

JC: I have a designer right now that I work with and he flipped out when I told him that his model is getting married.

DV: How would Armani handle that situation?

JC: He'd be like, "All right, cool. Who else do you have that's a 34-24-34?" The smaller the designer, I think it's more intimate.

DV: Do you just work with models?

JC: I work with the models, but I also work with the new photographers. At this stage, everything is new: The girls are just starting out, the photographers can be new, everything's baby. I personally believe I help mold photographers. I'm like, "Okay, I like this. I don't like the styling—try this lighting. This is what's worked well for me in the past." And they go and they work it out.

DV: Speaking about working with photographers: Do you have any advice for young models, designers, and photographers who are trying to get their work shot and seen? Can it be as simple as taking a good friend who's cute and shooting him or her?

JC: I had a photographer contact me through MySpace. Because I had booked the *America's Next Top Model* winners, he wanted to shoot the *Top Model* girls. And he's seventeen years old and he lives in Jamaica, Queens. And I was like, "Well, show me your stuff." And he showed me some sad little pictures, but he was willing to give me his services for free. So I said, "Okay, you can't shoot these folks just yet, but how about you shoot this brand-new girl from the Dominican Republic who doesn't have any pictures?" And he turned them out! And now we're paying him to shoot just for us. It was amazing! So, there is MySpace and there's models.com, which is a free service for models and makeup artists and photographers—all the agents are on there.

DV: What about for model scouting?

JC: Open calls. Every agency has an open call, where you send your pictures in—they don't have to be professional, they can be Polaroids, digitals . . .

DV: Jumping forward to Fashion Week, how do both large and small designers go about booking models, making payments—the whole process?

JC: Well, Marc Jacobs gets girls for trade. Smaller shows either don't have money or amazing trade, and I know it's harder when you're smaller, but it's a self-pitch. If you come at me and you have amazing clothes and I love it—and you have to have the whole package for me—then I'll give you a chance. You may not get the top-tier girl, but you may get an amazing girl that's going to hit in a couple of months or a year.

DV: Would you say that even though fashion is a business, it's very much about the people who work in it?

JC: Yes! It's all about the relationships. It's about how you meet people; it really is. I have a lot of repeat people just call me back because they're like, "I loved how you helped me out." And all I did was answer the phone.

DV: Is there one model who has really made you get excited, who has inspired you personally?

JC: It has to be Mollie Gondi. She was on *Top Model*, but she didn't win. She became a really good friend of mine. And I feel like we learned together, because we started at the same time together. I made my first big booking with her. She inspires me. I get excited whenever she calls. And I do New Faces, which never gets old or tired—it's like letting little babies fly out the window. Letting little birdies go because there's always a new crop. I never get bored, it never gets stagnant, and it's always moving. It's always a new place.

DV: Do you have any guidelines or how-tos for those interested in becoming an agent?

JC: It's all about interning, coming in, offering your services. My boss right now, he started as an intern when he was seventeen or eighteen and now he's one of the directors. I think everybody on my board except for one person—we were all interns.

DV: So don't be afraid to work your way up.

JC: Exactly. Don't be afraid to make or get coffee, because that's what I did at twenty-six. And don't be afraid to travel either— you have to travel, you have to earn your stripes.

"

HEIDI

SUPERMODEL HEIDI KLUM IS A STAR OF THE INTERNATIONAL FASHION WORLD. SHE HAS WORKED WITH THE WORLD'S TOP FASHION PHOTOGRAPHERS AND GRACED COUNTLESS MAGAZINE COVERS, AND SHE HAS DAZZLED FANS WITH HER WORK FOR VICTORIA'S SECRET. In addition, Klum's numerous ventures include her self-designed collections for fine jeweler Mouawad and for the popular shoe line Birkenstock. Devoted followers of *Project Runway* know her as the effervescent and always spectacularly dressed host of the show who whittles the competition by "auf'ing" one designer each week. Having a moment to talk with this stunning beauty about how she perceives the relationship of model and designer, and how important it is to believe in your work, was a pleasure that I am willing to share with you all.

KLUM

DV: Throughout your career, who are some of your greatest sources of inspiration? Who has really moved you, and why?

HK: I've been very fortunate in that I've developed relationships with some of the best, most creative designers in the world and been photographed in their amazing creations. I've worn Dior by Galliano and Valentino to recent red-carpet events; Roberto Cavalli is a superstar and has been so generous in lending me clothes for many special occasions; and, of course, I've gotten a chance to know Michael Kors through our work together on *Project Runway*, and he's been an inspiration as well. I hope I've picked up some tips along the way—I get inspiration from everywhere! For my jewelry line I get inspired by everything, from stylish people I see on the street to artwork to nature, or maybe even some crafts I see my kids getting into. Inspiration is endless!

DV: What do you look for in a designer's work and—specifically—what distinguishes whether it speaks to you or not?

HK: It's never any one single thing. It's more that I know it when I see it. When I have a big event coming up, I may try on several dresses, but I pretty much know by instinct when I've landed on the right one. For my everyday style, I prefer simple with a twist. I like polished punk—that's edgy without being too over-the-top or costumey. I find myself gravitating more toward looks with structure than to overly flowy, girly things.

DV: Which shows and magazine spreads have been some of your favorites throughout the years, and why?

HK: I don't do much runway except for Victoria's Secret, which of course is the mack daddy of runway shows because the production values are so high. In terms of magazine spreads, I can't pick a favorite—there have been so many that I love! A cover is really fun when I collaborate with the photographer on the creative direction—the chemistry really shows through in the final product. Some of my favorite photographers are Rankin, Ruven Afanador, and Robert Erdmann. I love going a bit off the beaten path. Straight studio shots are fine, but changing up the elements with hair, makeup, the concept, and environment all working together is key.

DV: How important is it to match the designer's vision to the correct model? What role does a model play in a designer's vision?

HK: I think the matchup of the right designer with the right model with the right look is incredibly important. I mean, a good model can make almost anything look good, or at least better than it would have on a hanger . . . but if a model's personality brings a certain depth to a designer's vision and the aesthetic is right on point, it absolutely shows. That's why I think you'll see some designers going back to certain models over and over—like with models and photographers, there can be a certain chemistry, and when it all comes together, it's a powerful image.

DV: In an ever-evolving industry, the game has most certainly changed over the past decades in how one can become "seen." Do you have any advice for emerging designers about how best to succeed in today's market?

HK: My advice is basically to work your butt off and hustle! Fashion is not an easy industry for anyone—model or designer. You really have to believe in yourself and your work and keep going no matter how many no's you get or how intimidating the path feels. If you're talented and get some breaks and really work to show off your skills to whomever you can, I really believe that success will follow. With a platform like *Project Runway*, I think the designers who are featured on the show gain such a leg up in terms of visibility and exposure—but those are just a starting point. The hard work begins after that, and whether you win or not doesn't matter—you just have to keep pushing hard.

IMAGE COUNTS

The process of working with a photographer to capture and help communicate a designer's point of view is obviously an important aspect of the promotional side of the fashion industry; finding a photographer who understands a designer's vision, or who can bring creative insight of his or her own to a project, is critical. Designers who have their clothing photographed use those images as a way to get their work and ideas out there for others, whether magazine editors or potential clients, to see. The images can be used for every conceivable promotional vehicle and opportunity, from look books to advertising campaigns to websites or MySpace pages. The purpose of photography isn't to create interest for weak design—the clothing should have appeal even when it's just hung on a hanger; it's just another way for a designer to entice people into his or her world, to communicate a personal aesthetic or a collection's distinct message.

For designers who are just starting out, it's imperative that they search in the right places for the people they need to help realize their vision. Hair salons, modeling agencies, and universities are all great places to begin building a collection of business cards that can lead to a portfolio of great shots. A new designer can easily connect with undergraduate or graduate-level photography students who are in need of practicing their skills by shooting what are called "tests," and with inexperienced models who need similar test shots for their portfolios. If a young designer takes the initiative to make those kinds of contacts at all different levels (not just established ones), the results can be both positive and lasting. The fashion industry is a very small world, and when there's talent to use, word travels fast among people in the know.

Today, the work of established fashion photographers such as Juergen Teller, Mario Testino, Steven Meisel, Patrick Demarchelier, and Mario Sorrenti—each a fashion celebrity in his own right—graces the covers and pages of every major fashion magazine in the world and sets the standard for contemporary fashion photography. Although a designer who's beginning a career doesn't typically have access to photographers at that level, it's important that he or she be flexible and try different collaborations, as you never know when something new could spark your

One never knows when past experiences will be useful: My years of dance training allowed me to give better direction to the model when explaining what sort of movement I was looking for . . . though it must be said that acting like a dancing fool isn't always necessary!

eye. Such was the case when I was still in college and a professor forwarded an e-mail to me and some of my fellow students from a recent-grad photographer who was looking to shoot a few tests with promising young designers. A lot of his previous work was landscapes and romantic environmental shots—not exactly what I was looking for, but his knowledge of light and composition was phenomenal, and so I decided to contact him. Only two of us responded to that e-mail and took the time to meet with him, and I'm glad I did. We soon hit it off and began discussing ideas for different shoots, new clothes, and assorted hair and makeup people. We did a few tests, and I just loved the photos—romantic, suggestive, and extremely beautiful—and quickly realized a new relationship had begun. Long story short, I ended up going on auditions for *Project Runway* a few months before graduating and used his photos during the interview process, eventually landing on the second season only four days after I graduated. If it wasn't for the timing, and the initiative taken on both our parts, I wouldn't have some of the gorgeous images of my

clothes, I *surely* wouldn't have written this book, and you most definitely wouldn't have all of the stunning photos in this book to look at—because Michael Turek shot them.

When shooting my collection for this book, Michael and I threw around many ideas and concepts in the process. Having worked together on this one project for more than six months, it made the brainstorming process a natural and progressive one, as we had literally gone through all the prior steps together. We both knew we wanted to shoot in a studio, as I wanted a clean, crisp background and Michael wanted to be able to control the light. The overall concept first began with an idea I had back in the sketching phase of the collection but that was tweaked once we had to consider the logistics of it all. I had drawn my figures in such a way that I imagined taking each page from a flipbook, lining the figures up on a page, and then dressing each of them in different outfits, but keeping the idea that there's one main movement—one story. My "flipbook" idea had the figures jumping off the page, grabbing a branch filled with leaves, pulling it down and letting it snap back up, only to have the leaves drift down, forming a pattern on the final figure's dress. A little complicated? Yes, I know, but I liked the idea of giving the girls movement and bringing in the nature element as well.

There were some serious logistical obstacles to this concept, however: We didn't actually have a way to suspend a large branch high enough so that the model could jump up and "hang" from it, and I thought it would be dangerous to have her jumping around in 4-inch heels. I tried to think of a less complicated way to execute the concept, which led me to the idea of silver metallic leaves blowing among the figures. As we discussed how to coordinate the blowing leaves and the movements of the figures (remember, we were working with just one model), Michael and I realized that we needed an experienced digital technician to help us layer and compose the final image. We worked closely with B. J. DeLorenzo, a highly skilled digital retoucher, before, during, and after the shoot to make sure we obtained the desired movement, mood, and balance for the entire composition. It was Michael's idea to bring in further visual interest by gradating the background with light and by placing the model on a reflective Plexiglas surface, ultimately pushing the viewer's eyes to focus on her. The final idea ultimately brings together the two main elements that I wanted to showcase: nature and clean lines; not traditional bedfellows, but I think the ultimate outcome looks amazing. The final image, which can be seen on the following pages and on the cover, is the result of our collaboration. **DV**

Michael and I worked extremely well together, checking our progress throughout the shoot to confirm that everything was in line with our original concept. It's important to see the photos as they're taken, as the images may not be translating exactly how things look in real life. Every photographer's methods are different, but it's best to approve images before it's too late.

JAMES HOUSTON

JAMES HOUSTON IS RECOGNIZED AS ONE OF THE LEADING BEAUTY/BODY PHOTOGRAPHERS WORKING IN AMERICA AND EUROPE TODAY. **He specializes in photographing the naked form, and his background in sculpture and design helped him develop the clean and graphic style that has become his signature.** His clients include Chanel, Clinique, the Gap, Givenchy Paris, and Victoria's Secret, and he has contributed to magazines such as Australian and American *Vogue*, Italian *Harper's Bazaar*, *Wallpaper*, *Interview*, and *Oyster*. Houston has also published several award-winning books of his photography, including *Raw*, *Rawmoves*, and *Move*, which benefited the "*Move for AIDS*" project. Knowing James's work well before I met the man was an excellent introduction. The way he successfully straddles the line between commercial and artistic appeal is one of the many reasons I admire him and his work.

DV: Can we begin with a brief background of how you got to where you are, and also how you became a photographer?

JH: I started photography in about 1982. I was a model in Japan and I picked it up; I had some spare time and some spare cash and I just picked up a camera and started taking pictures of my friends. So I kind of winged it in the best sense. I never did a course; I never assisted; I just winged it. Before that my background was in sculpture. I did ceramic sculpture through school. And I did a short stint in advertising as an account major, and then I was an art director. So that was my background beforehand. And throughout I've modeled as well just to make some extra cash. Then I was traveling, modeling, and taking pictures at the same time. So I sort of did that whole transition point where for about two or three years I was still modeling and doing photography at the same time.

DV: You didn't know which one you were aiming toward at that point? So good at both that you couldn't choose?!

JH: I never really, at the beginning, took it that seriously. I kind of just picked it up and did it. And then as time went on I started taking it more seriously and then realized it was something I wanted to do. And eventually I just transitioned into photography and went from there. I'm from Australia, and working in that market, I managed to get to a point where I was at the top of my industry there, shooting for Australian *Vogue* and shooting a lot of the main advertising campaigns for the designers and advertising clients. I was also doing a lot of work with the body. I shot the official calendar for the Olympic Games in 2000. I also published three books on my work with the body while I was in Australia. I have always shot the body as a subject, either in landscapes or as athletes or dancers, so that was something I was recognized for. And I also shot a lot of celebrities in the nude. About ten years ago, I seriously wanted to think about coming to New York to live and work, so I started working toward that. Because it gets to the point in a smaller market like Australia where you hit a roof and you can only go so far. Compared to the rest of the world, especially with fashion, it's always a season behind.

DV: Well, I love you Aussies—you're all so darn cute! So what came next?

JH: I had an option of either going to London or to America. In the beginning I chose America because it's healthier and the weather's a bit nicer. And London tends to be very raw, very edgy, and it's not very much my style. I'm a little bit more along the lines of classic beauty. My influences as a photographer have always been Richard Avedon, Herb Ritts, Paolo Roversi, Steven Klein, and Helmut Newton. And so knowing those photographers' works, I just felt that New York was the right place for me to be. Coming to America— it's coming to a big market, so you really have to be prepared; New York is like the pinnacle.

So I came into town and it was almost like starting again. It was very difficult. I didn't work for over a year. September 11 also happened at that time, so it was a disaster. After that the industry kind of just died. So I moved out to LA for six months and didn't really connect with that because I didn't like LA at all. New York is not like America to me; it's like Europe. I love New York. So I came here eight years ago and I work for my main clients—I shoot a lot of the main fashion for the Gap, and portraits and body and maternity, and Donna Karan, Givenchy, Hugo Boss . . . I shoot fragrance and skin.

DV: How many books have you done at this point? I loved *Move for AIDS*; the photography is absolutely stunning.

JH: I've just finished my fourth book. You can go to www. moveforaids.com and that has my biography on it, too. So, it's been a progression for me to get to this point. And I'm working now with great accounts, great fashion houses, great people, great artists, and New York gives you the opportunity to work with really amazing people.

DV: When you're working with a designer or a fashion house, do they come to you with clear ideas, do you bring suggestions to the table, or is it really an open, creative process?

JH: Well, some people get distracted, some are organized, and some aren't. Some know what they want, and some don't. It amazes me all the time that you've got a lot of designers who don't seem to really know what's going on. There are a lot of people around them and it's very confusing, and others are just totally organized and know what they want. I think that goes for every one of us sometimes.

DV: So as a photographer, being able to conform to what they need you to be comes in handy as a useful characteristic?

JH: Yeah! Exactly. As I said, it's one of those things where you're there to really capture their vision, utilizing the clothes that they've created. And to do something that works, also keeping in mind what their image is, you know? You can't deviate too much. Most designers have a certain look to what they do and a certain style.

DV: Do you think that at times a clash of styles creates something new and exciting?

JH: A photographer has his own style as well. So what happens is, a designer will utilize you because they like your style, and it usually aligns with what they're doing or their vision of what they want to do. So it's important that that works. Because if a designer is shagging a particular photographer and they just used them for the shoot and they're wrong, then it's not going to be right. It just doesn't make any sense. Photographers have their own style and they're good at certain things. Especially when you get to a place like New York, where there are 30,000 photographers in the city, and people really specialize in a style to be recognized.

DV: You started in this profession somewhat randomly, but do you have any advice for young photographers or models looking to get a foot in the door?

JH: The most important thing as a photographer starting out is to take photos. It's one of those things that if you want to be a photographer, then *be* a photographer. Everybody's at different levels, obviously, and it's a matter of getting experience and going out there and just trying. Role-modeling is key, in terms of looking at other photographers' work that you like, that you respond to, and just take an influence in that. And it's not necessarily to copy their work, but to take influence from it and try and replicate what they're doing so that you understand light and start to understand what "angle" is and start to understand cropping and start to understand how a fashion story is put together. How do you create a look that's consistent in light and feel for a fashion spread? And that goes for catalog; it goes for anything. At the beginning it's important to either do a course or to assist, even to do a third-assisting job where you're working for free for a really great photographer whose work you like—just to intern. And then eventually maybe you can become their second assistant or their third assistant. That's always a good thing. But in the beginning it's about really getting out there. And the good thing about photography is, it's everywhere. You know you can see it online, you can see it everywhere. It's easy to take influence from.

DV: What about equipment training when you're just starting out?

JH: Well, cameras are great these days. It's not brain surgery. Digital cameras are out there and they're fantastic. So it's really about getting out there and starting to take pictures. The other thing, too, is about working together in teams. Because if you're interested in shooting models, go to modeling agencies and start to test the young people who are starting out that need pictures. That helps you develop your relationships with them as well, because building a portfolio is another thing. You've got to get a stylist, hair and makeup, and a model. And the better the people are on your team, the better your pictures are going to be. Because I always say, "I'm a photographer; I'm not a magician."

That's the key thing. It's all about a team. If you've got a beautiful girl—I mean, it's very hard to take a bad picture of Giselle Bündchen, because she knows what she's doing. She'll take the picture for you. You just have to keep up. It's not brain surgery, it really isn't. And everything's been done. It's about just doing it again and doing it really well in your particular take on it, and trying to develop your style. Only about 5 percent of photographers really find their own style that's recognizable, like when you see a photograph and you're like, "Oh, that's a Mapplethorpe." I'd also say, as a photographer, just always work on your own personal stuff. Have a collection of your personal work and show people— that's really important.

DV: So they can see *your* vision, and not just your work with other clients.

JH: Yes. The other thing you realize, too, is that as you get more into it and decide you want to do it as a job, always realize that you're a product for anyone—whether you're a stylist, a fashion designer, a makeup artist, a photographer—you are a product. And in removing yourself from *you* as a product— putting your work out in front of you on the table and looking at it—helps remove the ego from the situation. Because the biggest problem with people is their ego gets in the way and they don't want to show people their work because of this or that reason. It's like, you know what? The more you can get your work out in front of you, the better chance you have of marketing it . . . seeing what needs to change. Getting other people's opinions on what they think of it and not being afraid to get that feedback, because that's only going to help you. You obviously filter what you want, but it helps you to really sell it.

DV: **Excellent advice. Putting your work out there is one of the hardest parts.**

JH: I think marketing yourself as a product is key. I've always done that. I always say I'm a businessman . . . *and* a photographer. I also work a lot on my personal stuff, my books and things, but I'm also involved with charities, and that stuff gives me a lot of satisfaction. It gives me a chance to work on my personal work and get it out there, but it also helps to really fill another part of my cup in terms of the community part of my life—what I want to do for the community, and that's an ideal thing for me. If I can do pictures I like to do and help someone or something, then it's great.

ETHAN HILL

ETHAN HILL HAS BEEN A PORTRAIT PHOTOGRAPHER IN NEW YORK SINCE 1998. With a client list as varied as *Newsweek*, *Entertainment Weekly*, *Rolling Stone*, *Food + Wine*, *Harper's Bazaar*, and *Blender*, the subject matter of his assignments has run the gamut from hard news to celebrity and fashion work, and everything in between. When I first met with Ethan, his calm demeanor perfectly reflected the contemplative, earnest photographs that he is known for. He's an honest believer in small details, in work and in life, so Ethan has been a constant sounding board for me to bounce off even the wildest of ideas. As a side thing, Ethan is a serious bookbinding enthusiast. He lives in Brooklyn with his bookbinding tools and his taxidermy.

DV: In your personal life, in your own work, what has inspired you and still inspires you? Do you go to a certain place for inspiration, or do you just look around and pull from random, outside sources?

EH: Well, I guess that all depends on what the project is. If it's a real story about a real person then those people are the inspiration. And I mean that the goal has always been to try to take a particular person's situation and illustrate it in a photograph in some way. If it's something like an actor or a singer, I guess I always ultimately try to take something from that person. I try to listen to the record, try to watch the movie, try to watch the TV show, and pull something from that that would make it relevant to that particular person. If it's a real person, then something from their real life.

DV: I know that you don't do a lot of fashion photography per se, but is there some element of fashion photography that you respond to?

EH: I have never pursued it, and it's sort of come my way by accident, and when I've gotten those jobs it's always been really fun. In fact, I was once told that I photograph women horribly. I've only done men's stories, and it's always been suits, which I think is really great. I like the whole dressed-up, formal, uptight sort of thing, and it just so happens that I've been able to do suits, and I like that. The interesting thing for me is that it's an opportunity to spend the day with someone and to try many different things. I will do twelve shots with someone rather than just two. And I've always felt that I had this personal rule to try to get three shots out of someone if you can, because they're not always good photographs.

DV: Oh?

EH: They can be good ideas in your head, and they can be good ideas as a sketch on paper, but they don't translate into reality. It's different people. All of these different things sort of come into play. Maybe that person doesn't like the idea, maybe the location stinks, maybe something in your equipment broke . . . whatever it is. I mean, it's really nice to be able to try to spend a day with someone, rather than just an hour. That's the part that I really like. I like to talk to people.

DV: Do you have any guidance for young designers, photographers, or people looking to build their portfolio or to experiment with new collaborators?

EH: That actually recently came up with a photo editor at *Entertainment Weekly*, and she was saying, "Oh my God, there's a guy who keeps e-mailing me these photos, and some of them are really fantastic . . . and then he sent me this picture of a pink poodle." And she said, "I probably get six of those every year, and why people think a pink fucking poodle is a great idea for a promo card—why does America love a pink poodle?" I don't know. So my advice would be: You cannot second-guess what people want. You have to stick to your guns and you have to shoot what you know how to shoot. You can't try to guess what the publication wants from you because you'll get hired to shoot the pink poodle anyway . . . but you'll be hired to shoot the pink poodle in *your* way.

DV: I see.

EH: And all those random, weird things come down the road, but you have to shoot what you want. It's like when I was first starting, all of a sudden I was doing all these house shoots and shooting architecture, and the only reason I was getting it was because there was one portrait involved with the owner of the house, or the owner of the apartment. I would have to shoot ten or twelve shots of these homes, and I would get to do that because of this one photo that would be with the person. So you get the weird job, it comes to you, but I think you can't try to second-guess what people want. And if you do stick to your guns, the problem with that is, I think you'll have a very up-and-down career. You're desired and then you're not desired, and then you're desired again, but I think that's the sort of thing that builds the longevity into one's career. The second-guessing makes you a flash in the pan, and it makes you interchangeable.

DV: That's the way that you build a career, by doing what you do best instead of trying to replicate what someone else does. So I think that's great advice.

EH: You have to work on your vision. And keep pecking away at it; obviously things change and you're influenced by the things all around you, but there's some sort of core there that I think is always solid.

DV: Can you think of a specific example of when you were inspired by something directly: a movie, a person on the street, or an encounter perhaps, and wanted to bring those inspiring elements to your work?

EH: Well, I'm fascinated by gesture. When I was a kid there was a book called I think *Body Language*. And this book was like a manual of "If someone pulls their arm a certain way, what does this mean about what they're feeling? If their legs are crossed, if their legs are spread, if they walk with a wide gait, if they walk with a short gait, what does that mean?" And that was always really interesting to me—gesture. Certainly, scenes in movies have inspired me, where you think something was either incredibly beautiful or really lame. And if it's beautiful, how can I replicate that? Or if it's lame, I want to remember never to do that. At the core of what I think is the most successful kind of picture I could ever make was the idea that you could look at it and you could say, "This picture is completely silent."

DV: Could you elaborate?

EH: If there was a feeling of silence, and the image of something between the expression of the person's face and the gesture and their body . . . and it looks like it was in the middle of something that was not necessarily definable. An example of that from *Shadow of a Doubt*, a Hitchcock film, would be this girl who walks up the stairs and here's this guy that she's just realized is a murderer but the rest of her family doesn't know—what is that pause and that gesture at the time? When she's at the top of the staircase and he's in that other room right behind that bedroom door, and that stillness of this girl standing at the top of the step and with her hand on the banister—how does that look? How do the fingers curl around that banister? And the light that strikes her clothes. Is that door illuminating her? Is there darkness back there? I mean, that's the stuff . . .

DV: Beautiful . . . I have goose bumps.

EH: And that's what I gravitate toward.

THE
SELL

SEALING THE DEAL

IT'S A COMMON MISCONCEPTION THAT A GLOSSY RUNWAY SHOW IS THE FINAL STAGE IN THE FASHION LIFE CYCLE, BUT IT'S ACTUALLY THE MIDDLE—IF IT EVER HAPPENS AT ALL. The idea of commercial success is rarely even brought up on *Project Runway*, until perhaps the final episode in consideration of choosing the ultimate winner; the show is usually driven solely by creative design. I think this is because when variables such as price point, distribution, and appropriateness for the market are too heavily considered, it begins to influence the design process too profoundly. Granted, the terms "sensible" or "appropriate" are so subjective in the fashion industry, especially when you consider the extremes some fashionistas go to in their quest to look stylish (5-inch platforms, anyone?), that I feel *Project Runway* can cover only so much in the time allotted. Is it better to have a program showcasing uncomplicated, sensible designs that are easily affordable and wearable for as many people as possible or one with more uninhibited ideas that inspire an internal reaction and cause you to sit up and take notice? I guarantee that the answer is resounding and unanimous, because how boring would a television show be where designers are charged with designing a T-shirt in different colors and choosing a width of black pants to pair it with . . . ahhh, how horribly mundane! The responsibility of selling and commercial success ultimately lies on the designers' shoulders after their time on the show, but it's the duty of the judges to support those creative ideas while they are still in a mentoring position.

Although the specific collection I've designed for this book isn't going to be sold in stores (the timing doesn't quite work out), I wanted to expose what those next steps would be. From producing a collection to showcasing it in a portfolio or look book, on the runway, or in an alternative presentation—it's all covered in this chapter. This is surely an exciting part of the design process, as it's when all of a designer's ideas finally become reality!

RUNWAY:
THE ONLY WAY?

There are many ways for designers to showcase their designs to the public, the press, and potential buyers. But before designers decide if and when to show their work, they must first decide if the timing is right. Choosing when to show can be a difficult choice, but it is one that must be made to make the most out of the situation. Some collections are best shown in a smaller, intimate setting to really showcase the details and cut of the designs, while others thrive on a larger, fast-paced runway experience. Even if a designer has dozens of potential runway looks to present, if the collection is filled with repeats and weak designs, there's no point in trying to fill a show just for the sake of having one; the message is always most powerful when a collection is clear and well edited. When a collection is well rounded and filled with pieces that are editorial and interesting, that's when a designer should begin to work toward the proper presentation.

Having the press capture a collection and share the images with the media is the most an aspiring designer can hope for.

Inevitably the first thought of many an aspiring fashion designer is of a glamorous runway show complete with professional models styled with amazing hair and makeup, presented to thunderous applause and a celebrity-filled front row, but they shouldn't kid themselves that a show at Bryant Park during New York Fashion Week comes easy—or cheap. Hundreds of designers fight for spots on the jam-packed calendar, and even then there's no guarantee that the right people will attend each show. The least expensive tent in Bryant Park costs around $25,000, which covers only the space itself and minimal staging and lighting. Add on expenses for models, hair stylists and makeup artists, dressers, and a photographer, not to mention the samples and invitations, and the cost of most shows can run between $50,000 and $1 million. A runway show is exhausting as well as costly, and while it's gratifying for a designer to walk down a runway to applause acknowledging his or her hard work, that by no means guarantees a good selling season. Aspiring designers shouldn't despair, though: As I've mentioned previously, using your creativity instead of your wallet can yield some very exciting results.

Although they aren't as well known or as large as New York Fashion Week, other unofficial fashion weeks and large-scale fashion events have been popping up all over the country. Groups of fashion lovers have been coming together to join communities of like-minded, creative people who are also trying to get their designs out there and support local designers. I think this is a fantastic way for young designers to build a name for themselves on a local and regional level, as the buildup of support will be advantageous when they jump into a larger arena. In fact, that's how I began. There was a group of us young designers who wanted to stage a large, community-driven fashion gala to help raise interest in fashion design in our area, so we pooled our resources and collections, pushed local media and sponsors, and ended up staging two years of very successful charity fashion shows! We contacted local hair salons and makeup artists, asked lots of beautiful friends to model, and hit up local stores to contribute a few outfits of their own, as well as local artists to display work in the lobby for a pre-show silent auction. We never had any intention of making money from the show—we just needed the exposure. Thus was created the perfect opportunity to pair with a not-for-profit organization to help bring support to the cause; we ended up finding a terrific partner in HIV/AIDS Services, Inc., an organization whose goals are to help treat those who are affected and prevent the spread of the disease.

Fashion presentations are a fantastic way for designers to showcase their work on a relatively small budget. Staged anywhere imaginable—from palatial ballrooms to minimalist, raw spaces—fashion presentations are not restricted by the traditional "runway" setup, so they afford more freedom for creativity and an opportunity to think outside the expected parameters. The schedules of editors and buyers during Fashion Week are long and exhausting,

and it's close to impossible to get the right people to attend a new designer's runway show, especially if the location or time slot conflicts with that of another, more established designer. Holding a three- to five-hour presentation gives editors and buyers more flexibility, allowing them to stop by as their schedules permit. A typical runway show lasts for only twelve to twenty minutes, and it takes place just once, so if an important person on the designer's invite list has a conflicting prior commitment that takes precedence over their own runway show, the designer is out of luck. Having a fashion presentation that extends over a period of time helps to better the chances of having the right people see the clothing.

The presentation format has other benefits: Editors and buyers can see the collection up close and meet the designer face-to-face. It also gives designers an opportunity to draw viewers into their world by creating a more interesting environment than a traditional white runway. I've attended presentations at virtually every venue imaginable, from grand ballrooms to old, defunct warehouses, from lavish brunches to intimate cocktail parties, and almost all have been memorable. Some of the spaces were decorated to enhance the mood (bales of hay and an old fence for a "country chic collection" or pumping music and spot lighting for a "sleek, sexy, cocktail-hour vibe"). Some shows were "static," with garments displayed on mannequins or motionless models, while at others models floated amongst the crowd of fashionistas, mingling with the guests and working the crowd as if it were just an elaborate party thrown by the designer. Whatever the setting, as with a runway show, the props, music, hair, and lighting should never distract from the clothing—they should only work to enhance it.

FERN
MALLIS

FERN MALLIS IS THE SENIOR VICE PRESIDENT OF IMG FASHION. Prior to joining IMG, she was executive director of the Council of Fashion Designers of America (CFDA), where she organized "7th on Sixth"—New York's organized and centralized Fashion Week—in 1993. As IMG Fashion's "ambassador," she travels extensively and is involved in fashion weeks around the world, including Mumbai, Los Angeles, Miami, Berlin, Sydney, and Moscow. She is a widely quoted fashion executive with many industry honors and recognitions, including being the guest judge on *Project Runway*'s Season Three finale. I was ecstatic about the opportunity to sit down and hear, in her own words, how Fern has tackled the numerous obstacles to build and orchestrate the colossus that is Fashion Week, for which she is know as its "godmother."

DV: Could you briefly explain your role at IMG and what it is that you do?

FM: Well, I guess I'm somewhat the godmother of Fashion Week. So this is now sixteen years of having created the first organized, centralized, modernized shows in New York. It's the big tents in Bryant Park. Putting that together for the very first time when I was at the CFDA as executive director. It all started because of a mistake and problems with how the shows got organized.

DV: Really?

FM: I'd just gotten hired for the CFDA job, but it hadn't started yet, and it was Market Week, which is what Fashion Week used to be called. And, typically, if there were fifty shows they were in fifty locations; no two things were ever in the same place. Everybody did their own thing. There was no sense of organizing, no sense of knowing how five hundred people get a taxi from one show to get to the next place and vice-versa. So I was hired at the end of March—and I remember the shows were in the beginning of April because we used to be at the end of the schedule, after Europe. And Michael Kors was doing a show in his loft space down on 24th Street, and they turned the bass music on, which kind of rocked the place. Things vibrate, but what vibrated was the plaster in the ceiling and it came down. It was Cindy, Linda, Naomi, and Helena . . .

DV: What did they do?!

FM: They just did this—brushed the plaster off their shoulders. Chunks of plaster landed in Suzy Menkes's lap and Carrie Donovan's lap and other people in the front row who wrote the next day, "We live for fashion; we don't want to die for it." And so I said, "Looks like my job description just changed." And so once I started at CFDA I said, "Okay, let's look into how we can prevent that from ever happening again." Then the next season, Isaac Mizrahi was doing a show in a loft space down on Lafayette Street. It was in the evening. There must have been twelve hundred people in the seats, because if you got a seat at Isaac's show you didn't budge, and before the show started the generators blew and it was pitch black—quite scary. And it took about half an hour to get backup generators and the show went off. So it became clear what our mission was—to organize shows, as director of the organization that represented most of the designers who put on the runway shows.

And Bryant Park was like the backyard of the fashion industry—it's the lawn for the industry. And so then the park was under construction and renovation, and we just wound up hiring a freelance show producer to help me put a project together. I went to Paris and Milan that next season to see what everybody else does. And then I got on the phone and started dialing for dollars and got Evian as the first sponsor, then got Anna Wintour from *Vogue*, then called *Harper's Bazaar* and *ELLE*, and then one thing led to another and we got sponsors, including General Motors at the time. I was just literally blindly calling people with, "This is a good idea. It's about time the American fashion industry got organized."

DV: Was there a personal drive in this? Because to me it seems like a one-woman army trying to tackle all that! Did you know it would be this big?

FM: No, I had no idea. But the office when I started there was about ten feet wide, with file cabinets and an answering machine as the secretary. And I hired an assistant when I took the job, and then we kept growing the office more and more and—as Fashion and Garment Center lore goes—you never move an office to a lower floor. You always move higher. Which we did a couple of times and got bigger spaces. And we did a lot of things besides creating the 7th on Sixth franchise at the time. We were doing the CFDA awards. We were doing Fashion Targets Breast Cancer. We were doing Seventh on Sale, the AIDS benefits. But organizing the fashion shows seemed like a no-brainer that made sense. When things make sense, then there's a reason for it to happen. It's easy to just push when you believe so strongly in it.

DV: And thank goodness you did.

FM: It changed the face of the fashion industry and certainly of the American industry. Because then we created so many systems now that people take for granted and assume were always in place.

DV: Such as?

FM: From the credentialing to the press list to a sponsor handbook. All of that had to start somewhere, with someone saying, "Why don't we put together all this stuff in a binder for the sponsors so that they know what to do, when it's due, who the contacts are? Why don't we charge the press a process fee to get their name on a list, find out where they're staying, where they could get invitations at the last minute?" That became the bible of the designers who show—you have to get the list. And it started literally—the first sponsors we had, I said to them, "Just give me a sign—it could be three feet by four feet, that's it. If you want to give a product, let me know, we'll figure out something." And that was it. And that's obviously evolved now into something entirely different.

DV: Do you still have a role in choosing who shows and scheduling when during Fashion Week?

FM: We do. Our office does. I work with Christina Neault—she's our associate executive producer, and that's her responsibility. So every season we often have to decide. Six people want this slot. "Help, Fern. Whom do we give it to?"

DV: When every season is a potential way for a designer to establish him- or herself, how is it possible for young designers to work their way in?

FM: We always have new designers on the schedule, young designers every season; I think it's become a hallmark of what we do at Mercedes-Benz Fashion Week. It's very much something that we are proud of. That every season people say, "Who's showing and who's new?"—it's the lifeblood of the business. And we always have at least three if not four venues, and whether it's the third venue or the fourth venue, it's always dedicated to younger designers. It's always a less expensive venue. And we also have some enlightened sponsors who are always looking for things that they could do—we are always matching them up to help to defray some costs for young designers. And the new designers have to grin and bear it. They take the nine o'clock space in the morning or the nine o'clock at night. Or they take it after or before a show that a more established designer may not want. You've got to start somewhere, and if you're talented and good people find it, then they get there. And they wake up early for it and they stay up late for it.

DV: For someone who's seen I can't even imagine how many shows in your life, is there a show or season that has spoken to you for whatever reason?

FM: There's still that moment when you get in the tent every season and you see it getting pulled together, and then the first sound checks and the light goes up . . . you know, you get little goose bumps. "Oh, it's happening again!" It's new

and exciting. But there are clearly some shows that were landmark shows in my memory. One I would say was Isaac Mizrahi's show—it was just brilliant with the scrim on the back wall, and seeing that and watching this theater unravel in front of you. There were shows that Donna Karan did when she was in the tents and had complete Harlem choirs singing and marching up the stage. There was a Ralph Lauren show one year when he did all these crepe evening dresses— everyone was in bright yellow, blue, green, turquoise; it was like an Academy Awards red carpet. They were just gorgeous. And the visual of them walking the runway and the way it was staged was spectacular. One of the more memorable shows was when Bill Blass retired. It was his last show in the tents and it was Hurricane Floyd in New York. *Women's Wear Daily* had written an article that said, "Will Floyd Flatten Fern's Tents?" I mean, we thought the tents would wind up in Pennsylvania.

DV: Literally.

FM: It was just a horrible season. The rains were coming down and the winds like nobody's business. But every Blass lady was making that trip from her limo and her car service with umbrellas blowing up the steps into the park. And he was pacing—back and forth, back and forth, with his cigarette in his mouth. And he said, "Fern I don't have to do the show, it's okay. I've done the collection; I don't need to do the show— let's cancel this, this is too dangerous." I said, "No, we're gonna do the show if it kills us! You're not walking out of here without your final show!" And the show went up. And he always had beautiful music, but this show was particularly wonderful. And it had all Gershwin and all the great American composers—it was so upbeat and American. And I remember at the end the lights were just very red, white, and blue. And it was very poignant, and there wasn't a dry eye in the place. I mean, he was Mr. American Fashion more than anybody for so many years.

And then of course the 9/11 season, when we were in Fashion Week and the world stopped . . . and we had to close down the tents. We all had to run out of the tents because there were bomb scares everywhere and people and security running around. It was the scariest. And then all these journalists who were in New York were from all over the world—they all covered a completely different story. It took us a while to get back, and fashion felt so stupid at that time. Like, "Oh, we do fashion shows? Give me a break."

DV: I'm sure. Speaking personally, which designers are you drawn to and why? Or does it change?

FM: It does change. When I joined the CFDA, I gave away all my clothes that were not American. And I used to wear a ton of Missoni way back then. And some Sonia Rykiel and Armani, and I just gave that all away. I said, "My job is to represent American designers, I need to put my money where my mouth is." I started to wear a lot of Michael Kors and Ralph Lauren and Donna Karan, and I wore a lot of Calvin Klein and Yeohlee Teng, because she's always doing interesting architectural things; I still wear Yeohlee. And that was the group—Stephen Dweck jewelry and Angela Cummings stuff. And I really started to just wear clothing of people I knew and liked, which was such a treat.

DV: And that's what it comes down to, isn't it?

FM: I'm not wearing something if I don't know them! And when you get through that head trip, that's pretty wild. And that carried through for a long time, but then . . . we're in a global world and a bigger universe, and once we were just focusing on Fashion Weeks and the tents and not just the American designers; the tents were never just for the American designers . . . it was the basis for it. I've since expanded back into Dries Van Noten, whom I love, and a little bit of Marni, Max Azria. And I wear a lot of Indian designers, such as Sabyasachi, who is probably one of the most talented designers in the world, I think.

DV: You obviously can attest to how this industry has changed, whether it's through technology, accessibility, or just more interest. Do you have any guidance or advice for young designers, whether they are in New York, other fashion capitals, or at home in the Midwest, looking to have their work shown or seen? Do you see a new outlet, because what worked for Donna and Calvin doesn't necessarily work anymore?

FM: It's a very different universe now. But it doesn't mean that for somebody who is really great that the opportunities won't be there—and they can become that big global brand. When a lot of student groups come to visit me, I always say, "Do you all really want to be a designer or do you want to be in the fashion business, because there are a zillion jobs in the fashion business." You know, for every Donna Karan on a label, there are thousands of people who are working to make it happen.

DV: Absolutely.

FM: So there are lots of ways to be creative and expressive and be a player in the business and not design. There are a million design jobs out there, so they have to decide. Do you really want to design because you love doing that, or do you really want to be a star? And do you want to have the ego that wants that gratification? Because those are different things. And it's very hard to admit that, what people want, but I think there are a lot of design schools around the country. There is now a fashion week in every city, not a trade one necessarily. Portland [Oregon] just had one. Seattle has one. Cleveland has one. Chicago has one. I think Atlanta has one. Palm Beach is doing one. And all of those are ways regionally and locally for people who are creative to get on the Web and figure it all out and finally go and meet somebody and show a collection and get out there somewhere.

DV: That's how I started: organizing charity fashion shows back in West Michigan, trying to create some sort of foundation . . .

FM: And this industry is like a pig sniffing truffles—they love finding it. Then again, who knows if it'll last. You gotta just stay true to what you believe in doing. And there are so many opportunities now. On the Internet . . . where people can do their own thing. They can get out there. They can make something and have it seen by thousands and millions of people. There are all sorts of ways to get known and seen and recognized. But the bottom line is, real talent somehow finds its way and people find it. I think it's a very right time for—

DV: New talent?

FM: Well, yes—for new talent and for talent, period.

PORTFOLIO
PROTOCOL Whether a designer is just getting out of school and hunting for his first job, or she's a veteran looking to make a career transition, a portfolio is one of the main components of that search. Because the main purpose of a portfolio is to help land a designer a job (and is *never* used to promote a line to an editor or sell it to a buyer), it should represent not only who a designer is but how he or she works. Its point of view should be clear, its message concise, and its sequence well thought out. A portfolio is a stand-in for the designer whose work it contains, so both it and the work within should be as well-prepared and professional as possible. In addition to beautifully rendered finished drawings, mood boards, fabric swatches, and press clippings of recent accomplishments, it's important to include rough sketches and relevant thumbnails from initial stages of design. Young designers often think that a polished portfolio includes only final illustrations, but the preliminary stages that show a designer's thought process also hold vital information for prospective employers. There are as many ways to organize a portfolio as there are to design a collection, but there are a few general guidelines that should be followed so that the work is always the primary focus.

I prefer my inspiration and fabric swatches to be displayed in a clean, orderly fashion, but if your collection and/or aesthetic promotes a more organic display, go with it.

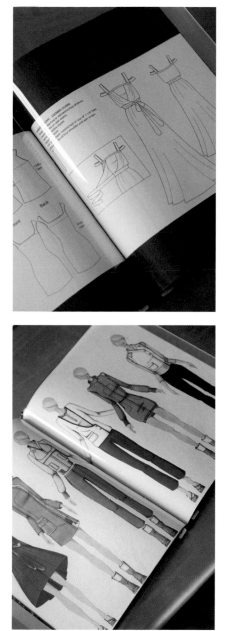

Be Organized Although fashion professionals are creative people with thousands of ideas to share, rarely can these ideas be communicated effectively if they aren't organized well. Finished work should be clean, free of smudges, and easy to view (with no complicated foldouts or tricky pull-out sleeves). A portfolio should be arranged chronologically so that the viewer can see the design decisions that were made at each step and how they evolved, from original inspiration to mood board to sketches, and how those ideas came to fruition. Pages describing a collection's mood and direction also draw the viewer in and help him or her understand how a designer thinks. These can comprise of any- and everything that led to a collection, such as photos of a fashion icon or interesting jewelry, pictures of a far-off land, or fabric swatches. Keep it two-dimensional whenever possible, as flipping open a book that has excessive bits and bobs hanging off its pages tends to look sloppy.

The page size should also be consistent. Choose one and stick to it: 11 x 14 inches is a good size, as it gives the illustrations enough room to fill the page and show the details in the clothing, though this is only a guideline. Another big no-no is for pages to have different orientations: If illustrations are vertical, mood pages and press clippings shouldn't be horizontal. It's a pain for someone to have to flip a large portfolio around as they look at it, and it only points out that the person who put it together didn't think it through completely.

Match It Up It's important for a designer's work to be forward-thinking, but not to the extent that it doesn't match the fashion house to which he or she is applying. If eccentric beaded gowns and frilly frocks are a designer's main focus, then a missy knitwear company probably won't be the best fit. Try to incorporate more subdued pieces if that's the case, or add splashes of color if the situation calls for it. Designers should be somewhat flexible when looking to move into a new position or company, to not be afraid to try designing out of their comfort level, but it's also important to stay true to their design aesthetic and philosophy, who they are as designers, as their talent is their most valuable asset.

Edit Well Editing is a crucial skill at every stage of the design process and shouldn't be overlooked when it comes to a portfolio, as a well-edited one speaks more concisely than one that's overflowing with sporadic and excessive ideas. Designers should show their newest work and aim for consistency throughout, with pieces that most clearly communicate their point of view.

LOOK, SEE:
THE LOOK BOOK

Literally thousands of new clothes are shown by hundreds of designers each season, so an easily accessible way to record and document them is for a designer to create a look book.

A look book consists of straightforward images of fully styled looks from the designer's latest collection, shot on a simple, uncomplicated background, or even images taken straight from the runway. They are traditionally somewhat small, usually no larger than 5 x 7, and can be bound for ease and order. Look books are meant as an accessible, quick reference for editors, stylists, and buyers—a way to effortlessly locate a specific top or dress, for example.

For my look book, I wanted to emphasize the clean lines and body language used in the final shot of my collection, keeping the focus on the clothing.

Numerous books are produced and handed out to magazine editors and stylists, who will in turn use them as guides when "calling in" looks for photo shoots or special events; it's much easier to request a top that has a specific page and style number associated with it than to ask for "the flowered top with long sleeves . . ." which leaves too much open to interpretation. Look books also remind buyers what the whole image looks like while they are on buying appointments; recalling a designer's personal aesthetic and style for a specific season can be helpful when looking at dozens of racks of clothes in a showroom at a time.

Look books can also be helpful when a designer is trying to build a new contact or get a foot in the door with retailers or magazines. If a designer is trying to get an appointment with a buyer at Barney's or an editor at *ELLE*, for example, they wouldn't just walk into their offices with rolling racks full of clothes; the first step is to see if the contact is interested in meeting. Sending a look book with a personal note requesting an appointment shows that a designer is organized and prepared and also gives the buyer or editor a chance to review the clothes before taking a meeting.

LEE TRIMBLE

LEE TRIMBLE IS THE FASHION DIRECTOR FOR GEN ART, A NATIONAL ORGANIZATION THAT HAS INTRODUCED SOME OF THE BIGGEST NAMES IN FASHION through their Fashion Week shows, presentations, and shopping events, including Zac Posen, Rebecca Taylor, Peter Som, Rodarte, Sari Gueron, Phillip Lim, and *Project Runway* Season Three winner Jeffrey Sebelia. Prior to working with Gen Art, Lee was the executive director for the now-defunct CLAD (Coalition of Los Angeles Designers) through which she launched the first-ever LA Fashion Week calendar and spearheaded efforts to create LA Fashion Week and the subsequent Mercedes-Benz shows in LA. Hearing from Lee how Gen Art can help elevate young designers through support and leadership made me feel a bit more relaxed about starting my own business.

DV: Can you tell us about what brought you to Gen Art: Did you veer from another career, or were you always interested in fashion and design?

LT: Well, I was going to be a professional ballerina, and then somewhere in my late teens I decided not to do that and essentially quit dancing, except as a hobby. And it was about the same time that I became obsessed with fashion. I was obsessed with the glamour, and Naomi Campbell, and all of that, and it just became something that sort of naturally grew. When I was about in my mid-twenties I tried a different career path—I'd lived in France and gone to school there and thought that I was going to be a translator. Then it just dawned on me that I loved fashion—I thought about it all the time. And so I took a career in fashion. And it was actually kind of a surprise to me. I thought that I was going to go into social work or work in the UN.

DV: Where did you begin your fashion career?

LT: I started interning at this new fashion magazine in Los Angeles, where I was living at the time. I interned for three months and they asked me to be fashion editor, to slowly take over for the fashion editor who was there at the time.

DV: In just three months?

LT: Three months. It was what I wanted to do, so I just jumped in with both feet. And I was really aggressive and really enthusiastic and worked twelve-hour days doing fashion shoots, not getting paid—just without blinking an eye. So I was just really motivated. And I started writing runway reviews for the magazine, and I started covering LA fashion in its incubation, its very formative stages. I was doing all this for free—I was just getting exposure and great contacts. I went to Rick Owen's shows. I met [fashion designer] Michelle Mason. I met fantastic people in the industry out there. And I started working at a fashion PR company because I wasn't sure that editing was what I wanted to do. I knew I had an eye but I didn't know how I wanted to parlay that. So I started working for the PR company with the hope that I would eventually start to work at fashion shows. And the owner of

the PR company was Lynn Franks, who started London Fashion Week. She wanted to start LA Fashion Week—she put me at the helm of it and asked me to start pulling together meetings with members of the industry. And part of that was getting this organization called the Coalition of Los Angeles Designers (CLAD) involved. They were sort of a trade organization of new and independent designers in Los Angeles that modeled itself after the CFDA.

It was basically like a forum for new designers in Los Angeles to get together and share resources, talk about difficulties they were having, trying to educate each other. They would do group shows. At the time, in 2000, they were very influential in the LA fashion scene because it was just starting to cohere. The Coalition of Los Angeles Designers asked me to be their executive director, and so I left the PR company and worked with CLAD, and through CLAD helped head up LA Fashion Week. So we started the fashion calendar LA, which was the first fashion calendar that was in existence. And it was exciting. It was like pulling together everybody who was really enthusiastic about fashion in LA at the time.

DV: But there was no organization.

LT: Right. And there was no clearinghouse for all of the shows that were happening. So as more shows were happening, there was more conflict. And so we created this calendar to smooth out all the conflicts, making sure people weren't showing against one another so that all the press could come to the shows. I sent it to every press person I could think of and called Fern Mallis and asked her to come out to LA to see Fashion Week—to see the shows as they existed at that time. And she did. And I took her on a tour. So, it was really about me working with a huge pool of designers, trying to get them recognition in Los Angeles and elsewhere. I've always gotten along really well with fashion designers; I've always sort of understood them. I kind of rein things in and I organize them, and that's my skill.

DV: So what brought you to Gen Art?

LT: Gen Art called me shortly after all this Fashion Week stuff happened, after I'd been at CLAD for about a year—they called me and asked me to head up their fashion programs in LA. I was there for three and a half years, and we started a bunch of new programs out there for shows for designers and did a presentation show. We started a big biannual sample sale for all these LA designers—it was really great. And then in January 2006 I moved here.

DV: I love it, because I hear from a lot of young, creative people from all over the world who don't have the community that Gen Art or CLAD is all about. But it all starts somewhere. For me, I started doing charity shows in Michigan for HAS, an AIDS charity organization. I did a few runway shows at a community theater, we sold artwork in the lobby, local stores were involved—and things snowballed. It has to start somewhere.

LT: Right. I actually think that designers who are from smaller towns that don't have as much of a fashion presence have to motivate themselves in order to get anywhere. They have to really pull together. They have to be tenacious, to conjure up this line and all of this motivation and all of this inspiration out of nowhere. And I think that really helps build a center for them when they come to a big city, and it helps them more so than it would help a designer here who just expects that because they're here, they're going to make it. No matter what, it takes tenacity, it takes a lot of hard work, it takes a *lot* of planning, a lot of organization. I feel like designers coming from other cities have an advantage here because they're used to people not understanding them. They're used to dealing with adversity in terms of being isolated with their interest in fashion. I always love meeting designers from other states because I feel like, to be obsessed with *Vogue* and Issey Miyake *and* live in Kansas, you have to have a thick skin! You know what I mean?

DV: Absolutely—I was one of them! So could you describe your role as fashion director at Gen Art?

LT: As fashion director my role is to work to find and help launch emerging fashion designers. We do this in a number of ways: We showcase them in large-scale fashion shows, "Fresh Faces in Fashion," and a show called "Styles." We also do a show in the spring, and that's primarily my focus. So in addition to curating and finding these new designers, I produce the fashion shows.

DV: And do young designers come to you, or do you go to them? What's the most productive way of getting their collections in the show?

LT: I think the most productive way of getting attention is probably to apply for one of our fashion shows. "Fresh Faces in Fashion" is a curated show with a selection committee, so you can submit your work for that. For "Styles," which is once a year, there's an application that you can download online,

and we review it with a selection committee of over thirty members of the industry. So it's a good way for designers to get seen. Even if they don't get selected as a finalist, a lot of times the selection committee will ask for the number of an entry that they liked so that they can write about it, or the fashion director of Henri Bendel's will ask for an application number and call them and ask them for an appointment.

DV: So even if you don't get the big prize, you're still getting some recognition.

LT: You get a lot of visibility, and it's a great show. And again, it's the only show that you can actually apply for; it's a fashion competition, which I think is great!

DV: What inspires you about a young designer's work?

LT: I think it's really hard to break it down—there are a lot of things that we look at: We look for quality, and the quality extends to the construction of the garment. We look for expertise in that sense. We even look for obviously straight hemlines—things that are as simple as that. We also look for quality in the fabrics. I understand new designers will oftentimes choose one fabric and work exclusively in that. It's their "namesake" fabric, it's what they love. It's what helps identify their line. That's fine. I understand cost is an issue. You can't go and purchase all exclusive, really expensive fabrics. But in fabrication, something to me that is especially important is, does it work with the construction? How well do your ideas translate with the fabric? How are *you* working with that fabric?

DV: So you look for cohesive ideas.

LT: Cohesive ideas, exactly, and I think understanding your limitations in terms of what you can do is also very important. A designer may love taffeta but their skills just don't translate well in taffeta. They'd be much better off working in cotton, stretch cotton, or some other fabric.

DV: Something that I've come to realize is that a lot of young designers try so hard to be the best at *everything* right away. Do you find it best to start small and focus or to show a range of things that you can do?

LT: It's very, VERY important to stay focused. For designers who are starting out, you need to show people who you are in terms of your line. You need to build an identity, and I think that in itself is a really important part of doing a line. You need to show people who you are, because fashion can easily be derivative, it can easily be repetitive. Everybody's different, with a different vision, and everybody's got a different personality, so showing yourself for your line is really important in setting yourself apart from everything else. I think the best way to do that is to be quick and tight—you can introduce your first season with five looks. Your second season, you can do twelve, fifteen the next. You can focus on a couple of different fabrications that work really well. I think the lines that I've seen that have done really well their first couple of seasons out have been really focused. I look at the line and, from the first piece to the last piece, I see the cohesion. I see what that line is about. I see what the look of that line is, and that really is helpful to me because it means that designer knows who they are. And they know their customer. That's what it really boils down to—for a designer to have a cohesive vision helps them to speak to a segment of the audience.

DV: Let's talk about creating a successful business once you've established an interest. Gen Art is obviously very supportive of young designers, but what happens next? Is there any support system?

LT: We do a business seminar series with the CFDA called "The Business of Fashion," and we invite all of our alumni designers so that they can learn about the business from a panel of experts; they can get a sense of what they need to do, what they don't need to do, what it's really like—in that way we try to provide them with a bit of education. We're also working on partnering with a production company to offer designers development services—patternmaking, grading, first sample set—all basically for free.

DV: Is that only in Los Angeles?

LT: Only in LA right now. It's something we're working on in New York as well. We're also talking to a trade show about doing a Gen Art space at one of the bigger women's wear or menswear trade shows for a season following participation in the show. What we're trying to do is figure out what a designer needs after they get all of this exposure through our shows, after they get all of this press, about what the next steps are. Like figuring out how to develop your line, how to get a sample of your patterns cut, get your first sample set done, get a second sample set done for press, get a showroom on both coasts or a sales rep that you really like and trust, get a PR person to manage all your press samples and learn about marketing. Learn about what stores need. Go to as many educational seminars as you can to figure out what buyers are looking for, how to navigate the industry—what Saks wants versus Neiman Marcus, what Barney's wants versus Henri Bendel's. These are really important things to know, and seminars can help with that.

DV: I know a lot of young people think that a fashion show is the exclamation point.

LT: Hmm, that ain't the end of that sentence!

DV: Exactly! It's an ellipsis, and that's why I'm trying to bring a little more knowledge to the forefront about what it really entails to make it work.

LT: Right, and a lot of it is not very glamorous. The fashion shows are important in terms of elevating status. You can get a certain amount of press up to a point, but a fashion show doesn't make your press, it doesn't make you. You have to have a buildup of press before that, and afterward you need to know how to use fashion shows, to be able to use the recognition that you get and use the press and parlay that into sales, and parlay that into getting bigger accounts and finding a showroom that's really reputable and getting a good production company, and the press that you get off a show will support all of that and get you to that level.

DV: Can you share any major common mistakes that you continue to see from designers year after year? Is there a huge pitfall that that everyone falls into? Is there anything you can think of to help guide the next generation?

LT: I think it's *really* important for designers to spend a lot of time on development of their line. A lot of the mistakes that get made are in production, and you don't want to get yourself to a certain point of getting recognition, getting your first store account, and then have production mess everything up and you can't deliver on time, and there goes that relationship with that store. Once you've created your vision, once you've decided on paper who you are as a designer, the next step is to work on development. Get a couple of boutiques to carry your line, a couple of accounts, and then really work on your patterns. Get a patternmaker and a sample sewer that you trust beyond anything. And that might not be your mom. You might want to keep it inexpensive and small, but you really have to do a lot of research to find people who understand the way your garments work and fit and what you're trying to go for, who are also very reputable— and that may take more than a couple of seasons. I think a lot of new designers think that it's all about custom work, and it's not. That's couture; that's something completely and totally different from doing an actual line that's in production and having a fashion business. Think to the next step—always, always, always. As a fashion show producer, that's what we do. You always have to be thinking about what's happening next. It's all-important. It sounds really boring and unglamorous, but from production, all of these different things will radiate: shipping on time, having a relationship with your buyers, getting it reordered—all of that stuff that comes from you having a really solid production manager.

DV: Is there anything else you'd like to share with our readers?

LT: I think it would be really cool for people to check out our website: www.genart.com. "Styles" is such a great show because it's so egalitarian; you can apply if you're a student, you can apply if you're a fashion designer who's been in business for three years, and we accept applications from international designers. The competition is really wide open!

THE BUYERS' MARKET

After a show or presentation, a designer must tackle the next step—the actual selling of the clothing. Inviting the right buyers and editors to see the clothing is essential, as this will hopefully create a lasting, mutual relationship with the buyers—who aim to buy great clothing for their customers—and with editors, who will hopefully feature the clothing in their magazines, giving the designer exposure. No orders are placed at a fashion show; that happens in the weeks following. Typically a designer will have his or her own showroom, or be part of a joint showroom that will carry the line along with other brands, in which a buyer can visit to place official orders for the upcoming season. A designer can also showcase his clothing at large trade shows, such as Coterie in New York City or MAGIC in Las Vegas: seemingly one-stop shopping for tens of thousands of retailers to peruse hundreds and hundreds of new collections, from mom-and-pop brands to industry dominators. There are both pros and cons to these setups, as being part of a large show ensures great foot traffic and lots of buzz, but it is also a competitive playing field, as there are literally hundreds of other designers showing their work in the same vicinity, making it difficult for one to stand out from the masses. A designer must decide where she can make the strongest impact on the right people, a choice that can often change as her brand grows and develops.

Finding the right store to carry a collection can be a process in itself. A designer must research the store's customers, policies, and overall mood, as well as the other designers it carries. There is also fierce competition among stores that cater to the same customer, so a designer may have to choose whom to sell with carefully.

Selling designs on the Internet may sound like a great idea, as it can broaden the range of possible customers, but in reality it is extremely difficult: Proper sizing for online ordering must be established, orders must be processed swiftly and efficiently, packing and shipping must happen correctly so as to not damage the garments, and inventory must be kept up-to-date and in stock—all of which can be extremely complex for many designers and become a full-time job in its own right. There are great e-stores for this purpose, however, such as www.shopbop.com and www.eluxury.com, which effectively play the role of the middleman, assisting in the complicated logistics of online shopping. In my experience, I've discovered that personal websites are hugely valuable for promotional use, as well as for directing interested parties to the right places: press contacts, store/selling details, information about the designer, and images from the latest collections.

DV

157

ELIZABETH BENATOR

ELIZABETH BENATOR FOUNDED HER COMPANY, ELIZABETH BENATOR CONSULTING, LTD., IN 2006, BUT SHE SPENT THE TEN YEARS PRIOR GAINING EXPERIENCE ON EVERY SIDE OF THE FASHION INDUSTRY. A designer by training, she was the fashion design career advisor at Parsons School of Design from 2003 to 2006. **She has specialized in recruiting designers for the fashion industry since 1999. In her own practice, Elizabeth is focused on the contemporary and designer market.** She takes care to approach her partnership with clients and candidates in a hands-on way, paying special attention to the unique needs of the designers and design teams. Always a strong advocate for designers, Elizabeth spoke to me about how she goes about placing them in appropriate positions to best utilize their talents and creativity.

DV: Could you please start by describing what it is that you do? What is your job title, and what does it entail?

EB: I'm a creative recruiter, and my role in the fashion industry is to recruit designers for my clients. My clients are a range of retail brands big and small, most of whom lie within the high-end contemporary to designer market. They come to me with the need for a designer, and they're very specific, like, "We need a men's denim designer" or "We need a design director for women's wovens." I ask them a lot about what the company is and what the criteria are, and a lot about the structure of the company, because when I'm looking at my candidates, I'm looking at them from a talent perspective, what's appropriate for their brand, and also their perspective. Then I have all of the designers I've known for all these years. I've been doing this since 1999. So if they seem appropriate, I interview them and look at their books and qualify them and then introduce them to the client.

DV: So do you continue to meet new designers as you build clients?

EB: I am always meeting new designers.

DV: Is it just because you live in a fashion capital like New York?

EB: It's because the designers that I know are constantly referring new designers to me. My business is completely on referrals. So the clients I'm in touch with are either clients whom I've been recommended to, or I've formed my relationships with them while I was doing the career advising at Parsons. So as far as meeting new designers, either they're coming to me referred or I'm getting in touch with the designers I already know and am asking them for referrals if it's an area that I'm trying to expand.

DV: What do you look for in a designer's work when you're hoping to place him or her? What do you look for that's a red flag, and what do you look for that's a sure hit?

EB: In terms of their portfolio, I'm looking at the range in their work, the cohesiveness of the collections—that's really important. I want to see that they've designed collections but I also want to see what the range is in those collections, and then within each collection the cohesiveness. And taste level; how much they know how to tell a story in terms of sharing the whole process from concept, thumbnails, mood boards, the flat sketches, the illustrations, and the whole package—presentation quality, appropriateness for the market. So when I'm looking at the portfolio, I'm looking at it critically from the standpoint of what is a good book—period. And I'm looking at it critically in terms of what's appropriate for my client. In terms of the person, being professional is the number-one thing. Though another big one is ego—it's a huge red flag. I really hesitate to present a candidate to a client if I think their ego's going to get in the way of their relationship.

DV: Which is not to be confused with confidence.

EB: No, confidence and someone believing in themselves is great, but they can't know it all already. And they can't be approaching the conversation with their colleagues in a way that is meant to trump their colleagues' work or trump their colleagues' efforts. They have to come across as someone who's autonomous and a team player. I'm most impressed when they have all of that and they clearly have a passion for what they do, and there are just certain people that I start a conversation with and that's immediately obvious to me. It's immediately obvious that they're hungry and they're driven and ambitious and all of those things, but in the most positive way and wanting to further the cause, whatever the cause of the brand is. And being resourceful is another really important quality in a designer.

DV: Were you ever a designer?

EB: Yes. I'm a graphic designer by training.

DV: What is it that draws you to this job? Is there something that you enjoy about working with designers or in a creative field?

EB: What draws me to the designers, and what draws me to being in this field, is that everyone I work with is part of the creative process in some way, and it's really the big picture. I was trained in graphic design with a huge emphasis on branding, and that was fourteen years ago, and I came to New York working as a designer and loving the challenge of being given a problem by the client and having to come up with a solution. I was designing print material that had to be appropriate for whatever the client's problem was but appropriate for the client and the brand as well. So then when I moved into design recruitment, I was in-house at Abercrombie, and what I loved about it immediately was that I was a part of the brand, and my effort to find them designers was directly related to brand relevance. So it didn't matter if I was looking at a graphic designer's book or a fashion designer's book—it had to be appropriate and it had to meet the company culture. It's partly the analytical process of problem solving, and it's partly building a team and just liking to be a part of the process that builds a team. So I feel connected to my clients. I feel a tight relationship to the client and what their needs are, and it's important to me to be a part of that and to not just stay on the outside.

DV: In your personal life, what designers speak to you?

EB: Bottega Veneta, Lanvin, Costume National, Vera Wang, and there's a brand in Berlin, a small brand that I'm so fond of, called SAI SO.

DV: Do you have any advice for young designers about whom to meet, where to go to, if someone wants to find someone like you?

EB: It's really just networking, period. It's the same way that if I was looking for designers, I would just talk to everyone I know in the fashion industry because you never know. You have to just get out there and meet the PR people and meet the stylists and network with your instructors if you're in design school and network with all of your friends who are designers and ask them if they know anyone else you can talk to. It's all networking and building those relationships. It comes really naturally to me, but it doesn't come naturally to everybody. That was one of the things I spent the most time on with the students at Parsons. I would say, "Don't pass up the opportunity to have a conversation. Don't say no to an interview because you've already decided you don't want to work there, when you don't even have a job offer yet." You just never know until you talk to people.

DV: Do you have any other words of wisdom to share?

EB: Something that comes up again and again with designers that I've been in touch with, especially the young designers, is they're so eager to start their own lines—so many of them haven't had the work experience, so they don't understand the value of having it. And it's invaluable. I have had so many internships over the years, and they've ranged from when I was in college having an editorial internship in an arts magazine to a public relations internship at a live theater to graphic design internships, and I've learned something from every single one of them and from every job. And they all have an impact on me. Every job I've had, whether I loved it or I hated it, I've learned something from it. And I think young designers are just so eager to go, and they don't realize until they've had a hard time starting their line up front, decided to take a full-time job, realized that they're learning something, and looked back on it, that that experience really helped, just to understand how the process works.

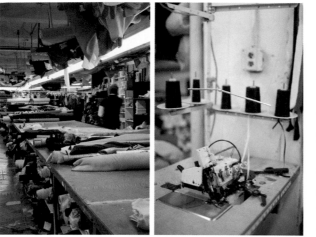

Grade pattern for sizes. How a garment goes from a sample size 4 to include a range of sizes is called *grading*. Most garment factories offer a grading service covering sizes 0 to 52 (or whatever range of sizes the designer chooses). The process can be tricky, and it should be checked extensively, as the entire pattern is shrunk or enlarged proportionately rather than consistently, with certain areas increasing or decreasing more (waist, chest) and others less (wrist opening, crotch depth). For example, the neck circumference of a size 24 isn't actually 22 sizes bigger than a size 2. No form of universal standardization for sizing exists, which is why some women fit into a size 6 in one store and a size 12 in another. Sizing is determined by each individual designer, with hopeful consideration of the typical market; unfortunately, this can lead to a lot of personal interpretation by the consumer. (Readers, keep this in mind as you shop for clothes: Never let a label dictate the size you wear; instead, focus on the fit!)

Create a marker for cutting fabric. A marker is a piece of paper that, through a digital process, positions all of a garment's pattern pieces so that they can be cut in the most cost-efficient and organized way, saving both time and fabric. A marker isn't as important for a small production run of a single item, but when producing dozens or hundreds of one design, saving $1/4$ inch of fabric on each shirt can add up to a lot of yardage—and money.

Cut and sew. Again, working with reliable professionals really saves a lot of time and energy. Traditionally, once fabric and markers have been carefully checked, they are placed in large stacks, cut, bundled accordingly, and sent off to be sewn. (Example: One pant design can be made in numerous different fabrics, so to save time the designated fabrics will be placed on top of one another in a large pile and cut all at one time.) If it's a large factory, garments are most likely sewn in an assembly line, with each seamstress focusing on only one or two seams before passing the pieces off to the next. This is why it's essential to have patterns that are well marked and understood by the factory, as one person isn't usually sewing an entire garment and thus individuals rarely know what the final product is supposed to look like.

Pack and ship. As mentioned previously, large customers like department stores can be extremely particular about how they receive shipments. Whether they ask for garments to be sent on clear plastic hangers, folded in boxes, or wrapped in poly-bags, it's important for a designer to adhere to their requests, as contracts typically stipulate that a customer can return a shipment if it doesn't satisfy their exact requirements. For this reason, most of the smaller design companies and/or studios that I know of pack and ship finished garments themselves. Although this can be a tedious process, it provides one last opportunity to do a quality-control check before the collection finally leaves their hands. **DV**

THE
POWER OF
FASHION

WHAT DESIGN CAN DO

SINCE BIRTHDAYS COME BUT ONCE A YEAR, THEY REALLY ARE MOMENTOUS OCCASIONS, AND SHOULD BE TREATED AS SUCH. So after months of preparation, not only was Anna thrilled to finally be wearing the new dress whose design we had collaborated on, but about the party that had been planned in her honor. All was going according to plan—dressed steamed, hair done, makeup touched-up—when suddenly the skies opened up and the rain began to fall. Luckily Anna had a huge rack of clothes to choose from, seeing as I had all of my latest collection samples at her fingertips. What better way to protect her from the rain than a coat with a plastic trench flap? To complicate matters further, it was close to impossible to catch a cab in the rain (as it always is), despite the fact that I had a gorgeous, leggy blonde on my arm. As a result, her Prada shoes were more than a little soaked after dodging through traffic and lunging for cabs for a good ten minutes.

MEETING OF
THE MINDS
We finally arrived at the party, where a delicious spread of cupcakes and sweet treats were on display, and a group of Anna's closest friends were there to greet her with open arms. The night was filled with "oohs" and "aahs" over Anna's dress (thank goodness), where I overheard such compliments as "How original!" and "Gorgeous color!" amidst the singing and socializing. Unfortunately, Anna found it extremely hilarious to continually answer the question "So where did you get your dress?" with the response "From Kmart!" despite my asking her not to numerous times. (Needless to say, she's so not getting another dress anytime soon.) Ultimately, Anna's birthday party turned out to be a wonderful time, and I'm thrilled to have been able to contribute just a portion to her happiness.

A nna has been such a dear friend of mine for so many years, and for her to straddle the roles of muse and client was a welcome treat. In her role as client for her party dress, Anna was very hands-on, giving me direct feedback, admittedly a new experience for me, as I'm used to having someone wear my clothing *after* I've already designed it. Creating a dress that marries both of our personal tastes and expectations really was a delight, but having someone who truly loves what I do wear something I've designed specifically for her is an amazing motivator and support system in itself, and one that I'm extremely thankful for. It's still surprises me to think that something I made with my own two hands can make someone so happy.

Throughout the design process for the collection, having Anna's image and persona in my head as a muse was a great way for me to stay focused when asking myself "Who would wear this?" as I developed my ideas. Knowing that there are women out there who dress to impress, who enjoy fashion for what it is and don't apologize for it, makes my job as a designer that much more fulfilling. To know that my ideas have the opportunity to be chosen, and worn, by some of the most creative, smart, stylish women in the world is a constant source of inspiration, and it helps keep me motivated.

DESIGN MATTERS When put to the test, the capacity for fashion to affect how someone feels, moves, and projects him- or herself is a wonderful thing. Although the combined elements of fit, proportion, style, and shape should ultimately dictate someone's fashion choices, it's often the loyalty he or she feels toward a brand that draws them in to begin with. Granted, that loyalty can stem from a desire for exclusivity, uniqueness or—the most superficial reason of them all—simply to look good. Oh, and I admit it—I'm right there, too. The power of fashion is strong. I can't help but feel pretty darn cool when I'm flipping through racks at the SoHo Prada store: the pumping music, the amazing space and the world-class fashion . . . shameless, I know, but it makes me happy! Have you ever put on a new jacket and just felt amazing? You stand up straighter; take a few extra turns in the mirror, perhaps?

I, for one, still get excited every time I find a new suit that I like—the way my shoulders square out, the slimming of my arms, that overall feeling of completeness—or a new pair of heels (no, *not* for me). I live for those moments of pure delight spent watching a girlfriend fall in love—or lust, I should say—with yet another ridiculously gorgeous pair of shoes from Bergdorf's. Suddenly the hair starts flipping, the smiles get wider, and that "absolutely horrible week" at work no longer seems so grim. The power of fashion to create confidence for a big job interview, an underlying sultriness for a special night out, or a feeling of individuality in a roomful of clones shouldn't be overlooked or ignored.

In the end, one can't forget that fashion design is an industry about ideas and people. Yes, there are tight deadlines, late shipments, canceled orders, unpaid invoices, long hours, intense expectations, and a seemingly uphill struggle to outdo yourself again and again . . . but it's also about affecting someone's life by challenging their perspective and overwhelming their senses. As a fashion designer I try to remember that, to some, fashion is a means of self-expression and a form of communication, not simply a way to cover one's body day-to-day. Ever-changing, ever-evolving, fashion has always been a passion of mine, and I trust it will continue to be for decades to come.

I hope you have felt the desire that I feel so strongly and have tried to express throughout this book. It's been a pleasure to bring you into my world. May it inspire you to follow your own dreams and aspirations.

Damir Vasović

RESOURCES

The fashion industry moves at an incredibly fast pace, so it's best to stay updated on what's happening right now. Of course the Internet makes it easier than ever to keep your finger on the pulse, so I've compiled a list of design schools and fashion-oriented websites that any aspiring designer or fashion enthusiast will find helpful.

FASHION DESIGN PROGRAMS

This is but a brief selection of available programs that I chose based on reputation and word-of-mouth recommendations. There are plenty of other reputable programs across the country that can be researched online.

California

Academy of Art University
http://drf.fashionschools.com/Academy-Of-Art-University
The Fashion Institute of Design & Merchandising (FIDM)
www.fidm.edu
Otis College of Art and Design
www.otis.edu

Georgia

The Savannah College of Art & Design (SCAD)
www.scad.edu

New York

The Art Institute of New York City
http://ai.fashionschools.com/artinstitutes/loc_newyork.php
Fashion Institute of Technology (FIT)
www.fitnyc.edu

Parsons The New School for Design
www.parsons.edu
Pratt Institute
www.pratt.edu

Rhode Island

Rhode Island School of Design
www.risd.edu

International Programs

Bocconi University (Milan)
www.unibocconi.it
Central Saint Martins College of Art and Design (London)
www.csm.arts.ac.uk
Royal College of Art (London)
www.rca.ac.uk

FASHION WEEK

(for LA, Miami, New York, and Berlin)
www.mercedesbenzfashionweek.com

COLLECTIONS

www.elle.com
www.firstview.com
www.style.com

TRENDSPOTTING

http://thesartorialist.blogspot.com
www.fashionista.com

NEWS

http://fabsugar.com
http://runway.blogs.nytimes.com
www.coacd.blogspot.com
www.iht.com/pages/style/index.php
www.vmagazine.com/blog.php
www.wwd.com

STYLING RESOURCES

Jed Root, Inc.
www.jedroot.com

ACKNOWLEDGMENTS

After working on this book for the better part of a year, the list of people I'd like to thank is quite substantial.

I'd like to begin by first thanking my amazing parents for all the love they've both shown me, and for the support they've expressed for my career in design, especially with this particular endeavor.

I'd also like to thank my amazing boyfriend and faithful friends, who were so patient with me (despite the fact that half of them thought I was writing a dirty memoir of my life). I truly couldn't have done this without you. Special thanks go to my best friend, the lovely Anna Scott, the most gorgeous muse a designer could ask for.

I owe the biggest thanks to the hugely talented Michael Turek. I could have written a thousand pages more and never come close to expressing the moments shown in his photographs, which reveal his keen eye and sense of style. Without them my words would have most certainly fallen flat. I'll cherish the time when I'll say, "I knew him when."

I'd like to express my gratitude to all those who agreed to contribute interviews, for their generosity in taking the time to share their thoughts and ideas about the intricacies of fashion with me. I must give special thanks to the incomparable Tim Gunn, for his numerous contributions and helpful insights.

I'd like to give a big thank you to the amazing team at Watson-Guptill, for helping to guide me along an uncharted path, and for their thoughtful and thorough understanding of my vision. I'd like to call out Timothy Hsu and Melissa Chang, for the creativity (and countless hours) they devoted to this book, to give it a "story" of its own; to the delightful Amy Vinchesi, whose intense drive and keen attention to detail never let a single word fall between the cracks; and an especially big hug and kiss to the insightful and always supportive Joy Aquilino, without whom this book would never have come to fruition.

Lastly, I'd like to express a HUGE thank you to all the fans and supporters of my work. Without the endless encouragement you've shown me over the years, I most certainly would not be where I am today. I thank you from the bottom of my heart.

INDEX